"MIG ALLEY" 200 MILES

Col. Royal "King" Baker makes ace, shooting down his fifth MIG over North Korea, Spring 1953. This particular MIG-15 carries markings of aircraft flown by Russian "volunteers". Col. Baker flew his F-86E for the 336th FIS, 4th FIW.

Color Key

 WHITE

 RED

 BLACK

 YELLOW

 NATURAL METAL

 OD

 BLUE

Photo Credits

USAF
US Navy
Don Garrett
North American Rockwell
Gene Boswell
M/Sgt. David Meñard, USAF Ret.
Col. E.J. Campbell, USAF
Australian War Memorial
M/Sgt. Larry Hendle, USAF Ret.
Ron Picciani
Fred Chapman
Don Miller
Col. H. Ross Collins, USAF Ret.
Air Force Museum

This book is dedicated to men such as Major George A. Davis, who paid the supreme price in the defense of freedom;

And to men such as Captain Joseph M. McConnell Jr., who gave his life to preserve the peace.

Many thanks to

Capt. Rick DuCharme, USAF
Mrs. Vivian White, AFM
Mr. Royal Frey, AFM
Ms. Anna Urband, Dept of the Navy
Major Pete Fernandez, USAF Ret.
Col. Vermont Garrison, USAF Ret.
Col. Ralph Parr, USAF Ret.
Capt. Cecil Foster, USAF Ret.
Major John Bolt, USMC Ret.
Brig. General Harrison Thyng, USAF Ret.
Col. Howard Tanner, USAF Ret.
LtCol. Bruce Hinton, USAF Ret.
Lt. Phil Janney, USAF Ret.
Col. Howard Ebersole, USAF Ret.
Major Alex Brewer, USAF Ret.
M/Sgt. Merle Olmsted, USAF Ret.
Lt. Leonard Plog, USN Ret.
Cmdr. Wm. Lamb, USN Ret.
Mr. Harley Copic
Mr. Harvey Brown
LtCol. Wm. DeMint, USAF Ret.
Mr. Keith Ferris
Col. John Ludwig, USAF
Col. Ben Preston, USAF Ret.
American Aviation Historical Society

for all their help

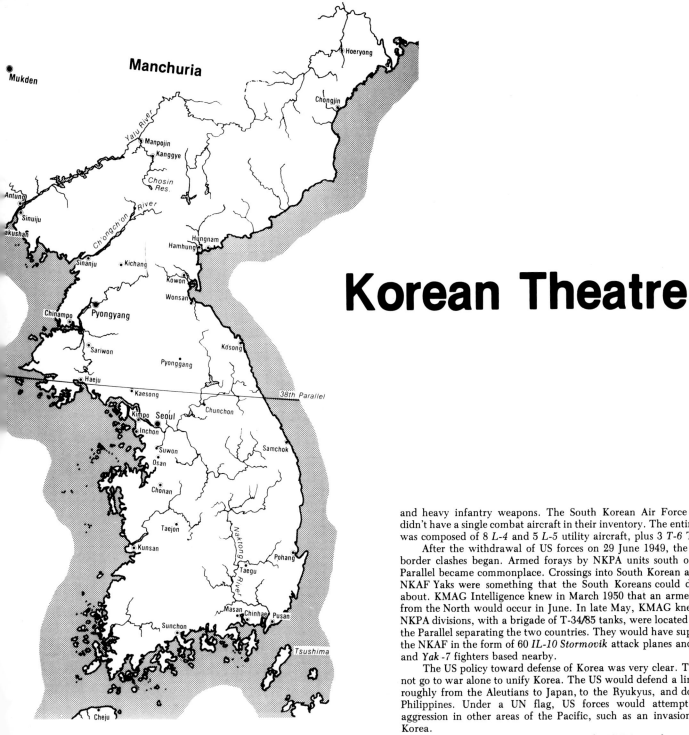

Manchuria

Mukden

Hoeryong

Chongjin

Yalu River

Manpojin

Kanggye

Chosin Res.

Antung

Ch'ongch'on River

Sinuiju

akushan

Hungnam

Sinanju

Hamhung

Kichang

Kowon

Wonsan

Chinampo

Pyongyang

Sariwon

Kosong

Pyonggang

Haeju

Kaesong

38th Parallel

Kimpo Seoul

Chunchon

Inchon

Suwon

Samchok

Osan

Chonan

Taejon

Naktong River

Kunsan

Pohang

Taegu

Masan Chinhae Pusan

Sunchon

Tsushima

Cheju

Korean Theatre

and heavy infantry weapons. The South Korean Air Force (ROKAF) didn't have a single combat aircraft in their inventory. The entire ROKAF was composed of 8 *L-4* and 5 *L-5* utility aircraft, plus 3 *T-6* Texans.

After the withdrawal of US forces on 29 June 1949, the inevitable border clashes began. Armed forays by NKPA units south of the 38th Parallel became commonplace. Crossings into South Korean airspace by NKAF Yaks were something that the South Koreans could do nothing about. KMAG Intelligence knew in March 1950 that an armed invasion from the North would occur in June. In late May, KMAG knew that six NKPA divisions, with a brigade of T-34/85 tanks, were located just across the Parallel separating the two countries. They would have support from the NKAF in the form of 60 *IL-10 Stormovik* attack planes and 70 *Yak-3* and *Yak-7* fighters based nearby.

The US policy toward defense of Korea was very clear. They would not go to war alone to unify Korea. The US would defend a line running roughly from the Aleutians to Japan, to the Ryukyus, and down to the Philippines. Under a UN flag, US forces would attempt to check aggression in other areas of the Pacific, such as an invasion of South Korea.

At 0400 hrs, Sunday, 25 June 1950, the NKPA struck across the 38th Parallel. Under the cover of rain and darkness, with a spearhead of tanks, they captured the city of Kaesong on the road to Seoul. KMAG had no doubts as to what was being attempted. North Korea, using armed force, was going to unite the two Koreas - under Communist rule.

When news of the attack reached Far East Air Forces (FEAF) Operations in Japan, they had only one duty to perform, the safe evacuation of US citizens from South Korea. American evacuees would leave by airplane from Kimpo and Seoul City air bases, and by ship from Inchon.

At noon on the 25th, several *Yaks* strafed the airstrips, completely destroying a USAF *C-54* at Kimpo. With this in mind, General Douglas MacArthur ordered FEAF fighters to provide air cover for the evacuation. *F-82 Twin Mustangs* from the 68th, 339th, and 4th F(AW)S would fly combat air patrols over Inchon and the Kimpo/Seoul area. At 1333 hrs on 26 June, an NKAF *Yak* bounced two *F-82s*. The *F-82* pilots, not sure whether or not they should fire, evaded the *Yak* and he flew back to the north. Tuesday morning, 27 June, saw FEAF commit jet fighters to the evacuation. 8th FBW *F-80s* would fly high cover with the *F-82s* low. At noon, the NKAF sent 5 *Yaks* to strafe the Kimpo airfield.

Korea - a small armlike peninsula jutting into the Sea of Japan from Manchuria. Korea is the strategic springboard for anyone wanting to control Asia. A country seemingly destined never to govern itself. Occupied by the Japanese from the turn of the 20th Century until the end of World War II then occupied jointly by the Soviet and American armies. Finally in 1948, the United Nations decided to unify Korea under a Korean National Assembly. The UN resolved that free elections would be held in all of Korea to elect a national government. But it was only south of the 38th Parallel that the elections were held and Dr. Syngman Rhee elected first President of the Republic of Korea.

But there were still two Koreas. The North Koreans, under Soviet leadership, were building an army, an army to be used in their own re-unification program. The Soviet Union supplied the North Korean Peoples Army (NKPA) with tanks and aircraft, then trained the North Koreans well.

When the American army left South Korea in 1949, they left behind an embassy in Seoul, capital of South Korea, and a small military advisory group (KMAG). KMAG would teach the South Koreans rudimentary military defense. South Korea didn't need an army, only a police force, so they received no tanks or artillery. They would be armed with standard

Lt. William Hudson - Pilot, Lt. Carl Fraser - Radar Observer
27 June 1950, F-82G, No. 46-383, 68th F(AW)S

We were circling over Kimpo when two North Korean fighters came up out of some low clouds and started after Charlie Moran and Fred Larkins, who were flying in the number four plane in our flight. The North Korean's shooting was a little better than yesterday and they shot up Charlie's tail.

My pilot, 'Skeeter' Hudson, slipped around and got on the tail of their flight leader. When the guy realized that we were there, he pulled up into some clouds and tried to shake us off. Fortunately, we were so close to him that we could see him even in the middle of the clouds. Our first burst hit the rear of the fuselage and knocked some pieces off. The *Yak* pilot racked it over in a steep turn to the right and we gave him another burst along the right wing. This set the gas tank on fire and took the right flap and aileron off. By this time we were in so close we almost collided with him.

I could clearly see the pilot turn around and say something to the observer. Then he pulled his canopy back and climbed out on the wing. Once again he leaned in and said something to the observer. But he was either scared or wounded as he never attempted to jump. The *Yak* pilot pulled the ripcord and the chute dragged him off the wing, just before the ship rolled over and went in.

The whole action took place below 1000 feet. Later we found that Moran had evaded his *Yak* and stalled out. When he recovered he found himself dead astern of the other *Yak* and shot it down.

The three *Yaks* shot down by F-82s on 27 June 1950 were the first of 976 enemy aircraft to be shot down in three years of war in Korea. Later the same day, 4 out of 8 *IL-10s* sent to Kimpo were shot down by 35th

FBS *F-80s*. It was the last attempt by the NKAF to stop the evacuation. Not one civilian was injured in the three days of evacuation.

Also on 27 June, NKAF *Yaks* shot up 7 of the 10 ROKAF aircraft at Seoul City Airbase, almost 50% of the entire ROK Air Force. The US now proceeded to give South Korea a small air force. Project BOUT 1 sent 10 ex-USAF *F-51D Mustangs*, 10 USAF pilots, and 100 USAF ground personnel to the ROKAF. Their job was the training of ROKAF pilots and maintenance crews, nothing more. Led by Major Dean Hess, the US pilots soon were involved in combat ground support missions. Since they were the only combat aircraft readily available, KMAG needed them, and the ROK pilots didn't know how to fly the *F-51s*. USAF pilots in *F-51s* marked by ROK symbols caused a lot of confusion. More often than not, Maj. Hess' pilots would draw fire from friendly forces, including USAF aircraft, simply because of the unfamiliar ROK insignia. The situation wasn't helped by the personal marking that Maj. Hess' aircraft carried - "By Faith I Fly" - written in Chinese!

The ground war was getting worse by the minute. NKPA tanks overran Seoul and Suwon even after US ground forces had been committed. The US forces were being sent in piecemeal, sometimes only a company at a time. Without heavy anti-tank guns, they could not halt the NKPA advance. The only tanks available were M24 Chaffees in Japan, which were no match for the NKPA's T-34s. Taejon, key to all of South Korea, fell on 20 July. General MacArthur told Washington that he might be driven from Korea.

While FEAF tried to take control of the air and slow the NKPA advance, Naval Forces Far East (NavFE) had the job of interdicting the NKPA supply routes. On 30 June, MacArthur's headquarters made all Korean airspace a 'free fire area' and FEAF and NavFE aircraft bombed in North Korea for the first time on 3 July. The next day saw the aircraft carriers **USS Valley Forge** and **HMS Triumph** launch strikes against the North Korean capital of PyongYang. After **Triumph's** *Seafires* and *Fireflies* had pounded the airfields at Haeju and PyongYang, *Corsairs* and *Skyraiders* were launched from the 'Happy Valley', escorted by *F9F Panthers*. It was the first use of jet aircraft in combat from an aircraft carrier.

(Above) Lt. Hudson flew *F-82E* #46-401 as well as #46-383 when he and Lt. Fraser made the first kill in Korea. **(Below)** This dramatic photo of the *Yak 7U* that Hudson shot down was taken by his RO - Carl Fraser. (Needham via Olmsted, Fraser via Olmsted)

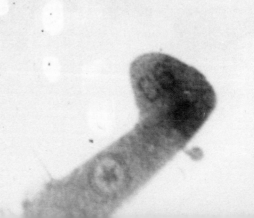

Lt. JG Leonard Plog
3 July 1950, VF-51, F9F-3 Panther, USS Valley Forge

The 3 July mission was the first takeoff and initial mission of the Navy in the Korean War. We launched about 0730. The mission was a fighter sweep over the airfield at PyongYang, North Korea. We were to sweep all the airfields and seek and destroy all aircraft in the PyongYang area. Quite a job for the eight of us since intelligence had briefed us that there were more than a hundred Soviet fighters in the area. We rendezvoused with the mainstrike force and proceeded to the target area. As we circled the airfield, we could see many enemy aircraft taking off. Finally we were cleared to strafe targets of opportunity. Just as I was beginning my strafing run, I saw a *Yak* heading for the runway. He was ahead and to my right and starting his takeoff roll. I banked over to my right and pulled up behind him. By the time I got into firing position he was well airborne, about 350 feet in the air.

As I was closing on him, I looked to my left and saw another *Yak* shooting at me. I thought "That dirty son-of-a-bitch is trying to kill me!" He had a perfect run on me but evidently had never shot at anything moving that fast before. I pulled up, watching him firing at me all the time. Then I saw Ensign Brown pull in behind him, very close. The next thing I saw was a terrific explosion and *Yak* parts flying around. Sections of the starboard wing separated and the *Yak* rolled right and went straight into the ground. We were less than 50' in the air as I passed over the wreckage.

It had only been an instant that I had taken my eyes off the lead *Yak*, saw the *Yak* making a run at me, and saw Brown shoot him down. I looked back at 'my' *Yak*. I was in perfect position and let loose a short burst from the 4 20mm cannon. I got a couple of lucky hits on his starboard wing and it just peeled away. The *Yak* flipped over and crashed into the ground. Brown and I went back over the field several more times - shooting up fire engines, control towers, a power sub-station. We got a large fireball and explosion when we hit a small fuel dump. As we were pretty low on fuel by this time, we turned and headed for the carrier. We returned to the 'Happy Valley' at about 0900. The first Navy combat jet strike had been a very successful one.

"Our Lil' Lass" of the 339th F(AW)S. The 339th was commanded by Major James Little, who also got a *Yak* on 27 June. (Trexler via Olmsted)

Lt. Leonard Plog shot down a *Yak* over PyongYang airfield on 3 July for the first Navy kill. (US Navy)

98th BG *B-29s* enroute to North Korean targets. SAC *B-29s* were the heaviest bombers used in the Korean war. (USAF)

B-26Cs inflight over North Korea. BC-532 is overall olive drab with silver fin and white tips on wings, stabs, and tail. Lettering is yellow. (USAF)

Still the NKPA kept rolling down the Korean peninsula. Taejon Kunsan, Yongdok, Kwangju - all fell to the NKPA. They were paying a high price though as the *F-80s, F-51s, B-26s,* and *B-29s* pounded them day and night. And Navy *ADs, Corsairs,* and *Panthers* interdicted their supply routes. With the Naktong River as a perimeter, the 'Pusan Pocket' was formed. It was all the territory in Korea still held by UN forces in late August.

The UN air forces concentrated on bridge-busting during the entire month of August. The **USS Philippine Sea** had been added to the NavFE forces. Along with aircraft from **USS Valley Forge** and **HMS Triumph**, her pilots blasted the bridges across the Han River near Seoul, and hit all the Naktong bridges at the edge of 'The Pocket'. *B-29s* and *B-26s* struck railyards, bridges, and supply routes, along with performing close support for the 8th Army. One such mission occurred on 16 August when a 'max effort' sent all the available *B-29s* to 'carpet bomb' some suspected NKPA troop concentrations near Waegwan. Intelligence had good information that a large body of troops was building up in the area. It was the biggest airpower strike in support of ground troops since Operation Cobra in Normandy. The *B-29s* dropped 3200 500lb bombs in a 3½x7½ mile area, creating a blast effect equivalent to 30,000 rounds of artillery. Unfortunately post strike photos and ground patrols concluded that NKPA forces had never been there!

With FEAF and NavFE aircraft destroying their supply lines and anything else that moved outside of the 'Pocket', the NKPA advance slowed to a halt. The fighter-bombers had all but eliminated the armor spearhead, and fresh men and equipment could only move at night. And not very well even then, for the *B-26s* from the 3rd BW were becoming very adept at night truckbusting. Flying single sortie missions, they would find whole columns of trucks moving, lights on, down from the north. When the NKPA truckdrivers started going 'lights off' at the sound of motors, the *B-26s* switched to Hunter-Killer teams. The first *B-26* would cause the truck to blackout. After he was gone, they would switch them back on just about the time the second *B-26* was getting in postition. The *B-26s* did this throughout the war, accounting for at least 38,500 vehicles, 3700 rail cars, 406 locomotives, 168 bridges, and 7 enemy aircraft.

In August 1950, the orders that prohibited UN pilots from crossing the Yalu River were cut. It was also in August 1950 that they were first violated. Two *F-51* pilots strafed the Antung airfield in China on 27 August - navigational error! On 22 September a *B-29* accidently bombed the Antung marshaling yard! And on 8 October, two *F-80* pilots shot up a Russian airfield near Vladivostok. The *F-80* pilots were courtmartialed, found not guilty, their CO was relieved (and made Director of Combat Ops at 5th AF). Harsh as these actions were, the pilots kept wondering what happened to the Russian commander who allowed his airfield to be shot up with absolutely no opposition!

12th FBS *F-51D* 'Tigers' being re-armed at Taegu. *F-51s* were an ideal ground support weapon because of their slower speeds and ordinance capabilities. (USAF via Garrett)

Map: Pusan & Inchon area showing cities including Pyongyang, Chinampo, Anak, Sariwon, Changyon, Kosong, Pyonggang, Sinmak, Haeju, Kaesong, 38th Parallel, Kimpo, Seoul, Chunchon, Kangnung, Inchon, Hoengsong, Suwon, Wonju, Samchok, Osan, Pyongtaek, Chonan, Taejon, Kunsan, Pohang, Taegu, "Pusan Pocket", Masan, Chinhae, Pusan, Sachon, Sunchon, Tsushima, Cheju, Ashita, Itazuke.

Inchon Landing 15 Sept 1950

8th Army Breakout 15 Sept 1950

Pusan & Inchon

Project BOUT 1 sent *F-51Ds* to the ROK Air Force. No. 18 is the personal mount of Major Dean Hess, CO of the ROK pilot training program. (USAF)

"Buckeye Blitz VI" from the 36th FBS. Capt. Joe Rogers got 12 tanks, 2 trains, and flew at least 130 missions in "Blitz". (Tanner)

The landing at Inchon on 15 September caught the Reds completely by surprise. It was a brilliant, and lucky, tactical move. If the tides had been a little different and if airpower had not been able to seal off the invasion area, events might have proved disastrous. But by 17 September the Marines had recaptured Kimpo airbase and were on the way to Seoul.

The 8th Army started to break out from the Pusan Pocket at the same time. *B-29s* pounded the NKPA defenses. With the 8th Army pushing the Reds out of the holes, they immediately fell prey to roaming fighters. One *T-6* pilot became the first USAF pilot to capture enemy ground troops when he dropped a note to some 200 NKPA infantry telling them to lay down their arms. They were to stay put until he, Lt. George Nelson, found a UN patrol to round them up. He signed the note "MacArthur"!

On 26 September Seoul was recaptured and the Inchon forces met up with the lead elements of the 8th Army. By 1 October, except for isolated pockets of resistance, South Korea was again in UN hands. That same day, elements of the ROK 3rd Division crossed the 38th Parallel into North Korea. It had been decided to unite Korea by force of arms - this time under UN control.

No sooner had the mop-up in South Korea begun than FEAF started moving units into Korean bases for the march north of the 38th Parallel. *F-80s* from the 49th FBG, 8th FBG, and 51st FIW went to K-2, K-13, and K-14 respectively. The 35th FIG *F-51s* went to K-3. Most of the strips were very crude and battle damaged. It wasn't unusual for the 49th's pilots to go through a set of tires on every mission trying to land on the PSP runway at K-2.

October was spent chasing the NKPA up the Korean peninsula. The *B-29s* were bombing the North Korean industries while Marine *Corsairs* and *Tigercats* did interdiction work. By the end of the month the *B-29s* had run out of targets. One *B-29* chased a single NKPA soldier on a motorcycle down a road until the bombs caught up with him. The end of October saw the capital of the north, PyongYang, fall. It also marked the end of the 'old' Korean War when Red Chinese *Yaks* strafed Kimpo. A 'new' war was just beginning.

At 1345 hrs on 1 November 1950 six swept wing jet fighters took off from Antung, crossed the Yalu River and attacked a USAF *T-6* and *F-51* flight. The USAF aircraft escaped but a new ingredient had been added to the war - the *MiG15*. A US patrol had captured a Chinese soldier - a 'volunteer'.

35th FIG *F-51s* on line at Pusan East Airfield. "Shoot-You're Faded", warming up, obviously has a replacement rudder. (USAF)

When UN troops recaptured Kimpo in September 1950, they found this *IL-10* that US fighters had shot up. (Tanner)

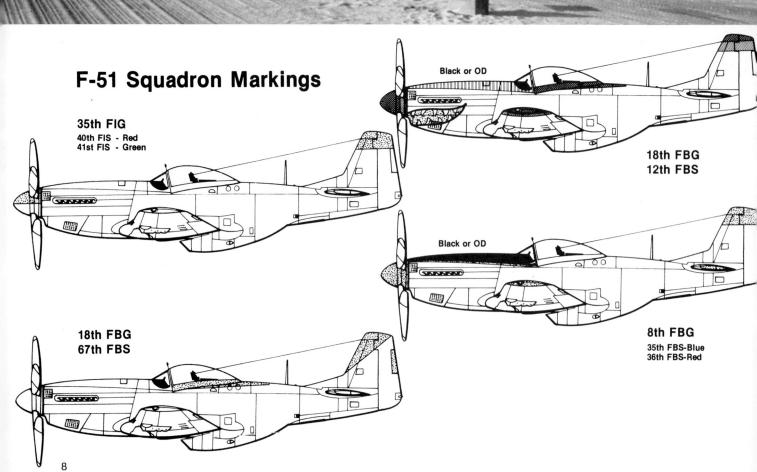

F-51 Squadron Markings

35th FIG
40th FIS - Red
41st FIS - Green

Black or OD

18th FBG
12th FBS

Black or OD

18th FBG
67th FBS

8th FBG
35th FBS-Blue
36th FBS-Red

**Capt. Howard Tanner,
7 November 1950, "Cousin Willie 2", F-51D, 36 FBS**

7 Nov 1950 - we were flying a Combat Air Patrol along the south side of the Yalu River. We had been briefed to be on the lookout for swept wing *MiG* jet fighters coming out of the Antung fighter base complex. The day before, Blue Flight from the 8th FBG had been jumped by the *MiGs*, but all had escaped, *MiGs* and *F-51s*.

We had been briefed for a C-16F mission (MiGCAP) and took off from K-14 a little after 1300hrs K time. We flew northward from Kimpo to Sinuiju on the Yalu where we turned to the northeast and flew on up to Uiju. Making a 180 at Uiju we started back towards Sinuiju when we observed 4 aircraft taking off from Antung airfield. The enemy flight climbed along the north side of the river and went on up into the sun, where we lost them. We continued flying southwest along the river at our assigned altitude of 10,000 feet. We were in combat spread and echeloned out to the right.

Suddenly Cousin Willie 3 called, "I have bogies at 1:30 and moving to 12 o'clock". As they turned into us for a firing pass, I called out, "Cousin Willie, here they come!" They were in an echelon to the right and peeled off one at a time as if they were flying aerial gunnery practice.

The first 3 *MiGs* began firing their 37mm cannon at us shortly after they left the perch - the shells looked like flaming tennis balls following a sine curve. The *MiG* leader had selected the worst possible firing position and the flaming tennis balls came nowhere near us. As each *MiG* passed in front of us, all four of us would squeeze off a burst from our six .50 calibre guns at it. The #4 *MiG* pilot must have seen us shooting at the other three so he decided to alter his attack. As No. 4 left the perch, he began firing way out of range. In fact, he was still out of range when he stopped firing and began a right turn. At that time, I called for Cousin Willie to break left and I turned inside the *MiG*.

I had everything going for me except the speed. But I was able to pull lead on him and fire about a two second burst. We were using API ammo and I could see strikes along his fuselage. The *MiG* driver immediately zoom-climbed to about 20,000 feet where he took a careful look around to

Lt. James Glessner (Above) of the 12th FBS and Major Arnold "Moon" Mullins of the 67th each got *Yak* kills in *F-51s*, with Mullins getting three overall. (Olmsted and USAF)

check himself out. It was then that I realized that I was alone - another radio call had blocked out my call for a left break. Keeping a wary eye on *MiG* No. 4, I located the rest of Cousin Willie and joined on Major Bucky's wing since Cousin Willie 4 was covering lead's wing now. I was clearing our tails and watching *MiG* No. 4 when the next attack came. After a second pass at us, the *MiG* leader picked up *Mig* No. 4 and climbed to position for the next pass. Instead of a quartering attack, *MiG* leader called for a head-on pass. Cousin Willie Lead made a slight adjustment toward the *MiGs* and he and Willie 4 scored hits on two more *MiGs*. After that pass, the *MiG* flight headed straight for Antung, with the *MiG* leader doing barrel rolls while crossing the river. We then returned to K-14 where we found not a single hole in any of our aircraft.

F-80 Squadron Markings

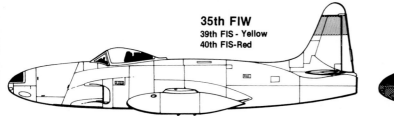

35th FIW
39th FIS - Yellow
40th FIS - Red

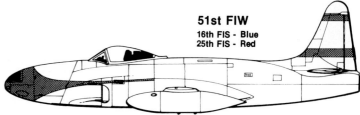

51st FIW
16th FIS - Blue
25th FIS - Red

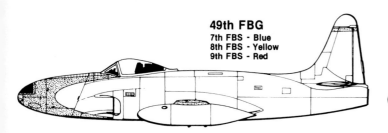

49th FBG
7th FBS - Blue
8th FBS - Yellow
9th FBS - Red

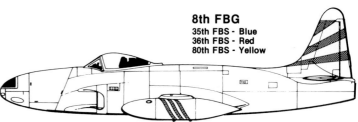

8th FBG
35th FBS - Blue
36th FBS - Red
80th FBS - Yellow

"Seductive Shirley" of the 25th FIS/51st FIW. The 51st was charged with air superiority in Korea until the F-86s arrived. (USAF)

Capt. Howard Tanner, who had damaged one of the first MiGs in Korea flying an F-51, flew this F-80C. (Tanner)

The next day, a 'max effort' was called for against Sinuiju, directly across the Yalu from Antung. F-80s and F-51s would suppress flak before the B-29s arrived, while 51st FIW F-80s flew top cover. In attempting to get the B-29s, MiGs came up from Antung. But first they had to get through the F-80 screen. In history's first all-jet air battle, one of the MiGs tried to dive away from Lt. Russell Brown's much heavier F-80. Brown closed on the MiG and poured a steady stream of .50 calibre bullets into him. The MiG flipped over and fell out of the sky. It was the first of an eventual 827 MiGs to go down in Korea. But to the fighter pilots, it was still very obvious that the F-80 was no match for the MiG.

Headquarters
4th Fighter Intercepter Wing
New Castle County Airport
Wilmington, Delaware

OT 370   11 November 1950
Subject: Movement Order

To: See distribution
In accordance with provisions of warning order, HQ Eastern Air Defense Force, dated 9 November 1950, and operations order serial number 28-50, Hq Continental Air Command, dated 10 November 1950, the following named units at the approximate personnel strength indicated will proceed from stations indicated to a theater of operations in a temperate climate for an indefinite period of TDY. Provisions of AFR 75-37 "Preparation for Movement Overseas POM," are waived except for immunization

Utilize APO #925, c/o P M San Francisco, Ca.

Capt. Ralph Parr flew 165 missions in FT-550 while with the 7th FBS in 1950-51. He returned to combat in 1953 and became a double ace flying F-86Fs with the 4th FIW. (USAF)

With those few words, the pilots and planes of the 4th FIW went to Korea. The pilots of the 4th were probably the best jet fighter pilots in the USAF. Many were combat veterans from WWII and all had extensive jet training, including 1½ years in the F-86. Just prior to leaving for the west coast, the best aircraft from the other three F-86 wings in ConUS were traded to the 4th for some of their older models. The 334th and 335th FIS then flew to San Diego. Planes and crews were loaded on the jeep carrier **USS Cape Esperance.** The 336th FIS went to San Francisco and loaded on a tanker, arriving at Kisarazu, Japan, about two weeks before the other two units.

At the same time, USAF ordered the 27th FEG, and their new F-84Es, to Korea by way of a jeep carrier. Additionally, 3 RB-45Cs, Detachment A of the 84th BS(L), was sent to Misawa AB, Japan. Recon aircraft had been taking a beating from the MiGs. Perhaps the fast RB-45s might be the answer. But the RB-45s couldn't handle the MiGs either and had to have fighter escort on any mission onto MiG Alley.

When the 336th FIS off-loaded their F-86s, they found to their dismay that the aircraft hadn't been adequately waterproofed. Salt water corrosion had taken such a toll that only seven aircraft could be made combat ready. The F-84Es were in a similar state but did manage to get one squadron operational. They flew their first combat mission from K-2 on 6 December 1950. The 336th FIS, 7 aircraft strong, went to K-14 where they started combat operations on 15 December.

4th FIG *F-86s* **went to Korea on the jeep carrier USS Cape Esperance, seen here at Kisarazu, Japan. (NAA)**

16 December 1950. The Korean Winter prevented the first combat sweep of *MiG* **Alley by the 4th Wing** *Sabres.* **(Hinton)**

The weather cleared on 17 December and the 336th FIS flew their first *MiG* sweep. LtCol. Bruce Hinton got the first *MiG* by a *Sabre* pilot on this day. (Hinton)

LtCol. Bruce Hinton
17 December 1950, "Baker Lead", 336 FS, F-86A,
No. 49-1236

The Fourth Fighter Group went into Korea on 13 December 1950, with seven *F-86A Sabres*. Our first mission was an orientation flight over North Korea on December 15th but we had no contact with the enemy. December 16th we were closed in by weather so we talked to some *F-80* jocks who had encountered the *MiGs*. One told about how he had shot one down when the *MiG* flew into the *F-80* formation at low speed and altitude. It was Lt. Russell Brown, from the 51st FIW.

These pilots described the aircraft with its high horizontal tail, wings swept a little different than the *F-86's*, and the stub nose. Speed, they told us, was about like the *F-80* but they had no news on the armament or maneuverability of the *MiG.*

December 17th - the weather moved on leaving a heavy layer of snow on the runways at Kimpo. The first combat mission by the 4th FG was scheduled for the afternoon. After the runway had been plowed by what looked like early World War I trucks, Baker Flight pulled off the parking ramp onto the active. We were carrying the normal combat load for an *F-86* - two 120 gallon external tanks and 2000 rounds of HEI ammunition for the six .50 calibre guns.

1405K (Korean Local Time), Baker 1 and 2 rolled down the K-14 runway, followed in six seconds by Baker 3 and 4. Join-up, change channels, check in and I slid rudder pedals to fishtail, the signal for combat spread. We climbed out to 25,000 ft., heading on a direct course to Sinuiju, about 200 miles away. Crossing PyongYang, we tested our guns. We had clear sky with visibility all the way to Moscow.

Approaching Sinuiju, we dropped our speed to that of an *F-80* on cruise setting, hoping to tease them out. We knew they had a GCI of some type and hoped they would vector the *MiGs* to intercept the invading '*F-80s*'. About 5 miles south of Sinuiju, we turned right in combat spread and started to patrol parallel with the Yalu River. The sun was high and behind us.

"Baker Lead, I have bogies at 9 o'clock low and crossing", came from Baker 2. Slightly below us at about 20,000ft., I saw a flight of four swept wing fighters moving very fast, crossing our track about a mile ahead and climbing. It was a completely startling sight! They were in loose finger-four formation. Their speed was astonishing. I punched the mike button, "Baker flight, drop tanks!" No reply, a dead transmitter. I tried again. Still dead. Again! Nothing! It was clear that my radio had failed.

The *MiGs* went across to our right and started a climbing turn back to us. No time to lose! I punched off the tanks and went to full military on the throttle. A hard pull into their turn brought me in at their 5 o'clock and closing. They were climbing to meet us; we were diving slightly on them. I picked the *MiG* leader to attack. Baker 3 and 4 were taking on *MiGs* 3 and 4. As I closed to within 4,000 feet, the *MiGs* suddenly cleaned their external tanks. The tanks separated, twisting sideways and flipping end over end, trailing a plume of white spray.

As I moved to the 6 o'clock position on the *MiG* leader, I started checking my airspeed. The *F-86A* is redlined at .95 mach and my machmeter was well beyond the redline. At this point, the *MiG* flight began to spread. Out of the corner of my eye, the element (*MiG* 3 and 4) seemed to be breaking

13

away from the lead aircraft. *MiG* 1 and 2 slowly rolled from a climbing turn into a level left bank with the lead *MiG* going slightly high. That settled it, and I picked up the closest *MiG*, the leader's wingman, put my pipper on his left fuselage about where the fuel tank should be and closed the range. The gunsight had stadiametric ranging and I set the sight for a 30' span.

At 1500 feet, I let go a short burst and saw strikes against the middle left fuselage and from the right wing where the bullet pattern had sprayed across. The holes appeared to cause some kind of leaks as either smoke or fuel spray was streaming back.

The lead *MiG* had drifted higher, sitting about 45° to the right and about 200 feet higher than No. 2 and myself. Thinking "Could the *MiG* leader position himself to hit me from where he was or where he was going? He could be about to work a defensive split (as US pilots would do) to draw my attention away, or to pull off a high attack on my wingman and myself. Wingman? Baker 2 was not with me! Then I knew. When we had initiated the break into the *MiGs*, I had momentarily straightened out to work with my radio. Baker 2, 3 and 4 had continued the break coming around on the *MiG* element that had been crossing. My pause had caused our separation. I was alone!

I decided to watch the *MiG* leader, but work on No. 2, who suddenly popped his speed brakes, then retracted them immediately. That momentary drag increased my closure rate and I put my pipper on his tailpipe. My airplane abruptly began a violent twisting and bouncing in his jet wash, so I slid off to the inside slightly, clearing the turbulence. Range down to about 800 feet. I pressed the trigger for a good long burst into his engine. Pieces flew out, smoke filled the tailpipe, and the flame lengthened out the opening. He lost airspeed at once and I put out my speed brakes, throttled to idle and moved in closer to him. We hung there in the sky, turning left, with my airplane tight against his underside in a show formation. We were about 5 feet apart and I got a good close view of his *MiG*. It was a beautiful, sports car of a fighter. The silver aluminum of pure metal was clean and gleaming, no dirt on the underside from mud thrown back from its wheels. It looked like a first class airplane.

After hanging there for what seemed like a long time, I moved out and over him looking for the other *MiGs*. None in sight, we were all alone. The *MiG* was losing altitude very fast in a 45° left bank at low airspeed. I moved farther to his inside, now about 2,000 feet above and thought, "Why doesn't he blow?" His airplane was smoking out of several places and fire was still coming out of the tailpipe. "OK! I'll finish him!" In a diving left turn, I put the pipper on the forward fuselage and fired a long, long burst. The API flashed and twinkled on the left and right wing roots and in the cockpit area. He rolled on his back and dived. trailing smoke and flame, crashing into the snow covered earth below. There was no parachute.

Baker 3 and 4 had run the other *MiG* element back into Manchuria and were wondering whether the airplane they had seen going down was a *MiG* or me. Baker 2 kept asking everyone where Baker Lead was. No one knew, and I couldn't tell them. It seemed a long way back to K-14 alone in the brightness of the Korean sky. Some 20 minutes later, I brought the *Sabre* down a long fast dive over the active runway at Kimpo. Leveling off at slightly over 500 knots, I did the traditional victory roll indicating one *MiG* down (and 791 to go!).

Lt. Jacob Kratt shot down two *MiGs* on 23 January 1951, and later got a *Yak*, while flying with the 523rd FES. (Esposito)

F-84Es of the 27th FEW were also committed to the war at the same time as the F-86s. F-84Es, faster and more nimble than the F-80, had a better chance against the MiG. (USAF)

The *Sabres* were run out of Kimpo on 2 January 1951 by the advance of the CCF ground forces. The CCF had mauled the UN troops and had forced sea evacuations of Marine, ROK, and US Army units from Hungnam. At the Chosin Reservoir, the 1st Marine Division was completely encircled and had to fight and march for thirteen straight days before they broke out. *C-119s* and *C-47s* supplied them by air while Marine *Corsairs* orbited overhead. At any sign of trouble the Marine *Corsairs* looked after their own. The Marines fought their way out and brought all their wounded and dead with them. By the end of January, the CCF had pushed the UN troops back across the 38th, capturing Seoul, Kimpo, and Suwon in the process.

The fighter-bombers pounded the CCF throughout the daylight hours, while *B-26s* did the job at night. The 4th FIW *Sabres* had to retire to Japan and couldn't fly MiGCAP patrols due to their limited range. It would be almost spring before the *F-86s* returned to Korea.

Before leaving Korea, the *Sabres* had done a good job of controlling the *MiGs*. Now, with the *F-86s* in Japan, the *MiGs* appeared further and further south. With clear ascendency over the *F-80s* and *F-84s*, the *MiGs* got braver, and a little reckless. They ran into a buzzsaw on 21 January when they attacked some 523rd FES *F-84s*. The CO of the 523rd, LtCol. Wm. Bertram, found a *MiG* in his sights and shot it down. Two days later, a 'max effort' of 33 *F-84s* was sent to Sinuiju to beat up the airfield. Two flights went in on the deck and worked over the field while the other

six flights flew MiGCAP. When the dust had cleared, the 27th had four more *MiGs*, including two by Lt. Jacob Kratt, 3 probables and 4 damaged with no *F-84* losses!

By 10 February, both Suwon and Kimpo were back in UN control. The CCF drive had stalled and they had pulled back to defensive positions along the 38th Parallel. The 334th brought its *Sabres* back to Korea, moving to K-2 on 22 February. At this time, neither K-13 or 14 was serviceable as a jet fighter base, although the *F-51s* were using both. With the *Sabres* flying from K-2, they could only range out as far as PyongYang. This meant that any *B-29* raids into the *MiG* Alley region had to be escorted by *F-80s*. On 1 March, the *B-29s* were badly mauled by the *MiGs* when they attempted to bomb the Yalu bridges. A bad headwind cut the *F-80s* escort time to but a few minutes, and no time at all over target. *MiGs* attacked the *B-29* force and badly damaged 10 of the bombers, 3 so bad that they never flew again.

A hurry up order went out and the *F-86s* moved back into Suwon on 6 March. The field was not exactly in tip top shape. Col. Ben Preston, CO of the 4th FIW, recalls the conditions:

We were based at Suwon and shared a single narrow asphalt strip with an *F-80* outfit. The runway had only one taxi strip entrance which made recovery after a mission very hairy indeed. We landed on one side, swung around and taxied up the other side while aircraft kept coming in to land.

LtCol. William Bertram, CO of the 523rd, also got a MiG when he led the squadron to Sinuiju on 21 January 1951. (Balogh via Menard)

After being driven from Korea by the advancing Chinese in January, the F-86s returned to Taegu in March 1951. However, they could not fly MiG sweeps from Taegu due to the range. (Tanner)

Our wingtip clearance was maybe ten feet. Remember that some aircraft had battle damage - some were down to zero fuel and barely under control. It was almost unbelievable to new pilots fresh from the states.

Operating from Suwon, the Sabres could once again patrol MiG Alley. And Sabre patrols were costly to the Reds. 8 MiGs went down on 3/4 April, 4 more on 12 April, and another 4 on 22 April. The MiGs were trying to stop the B-29s which were systematically knocking out the Yalu bridges and airfields.

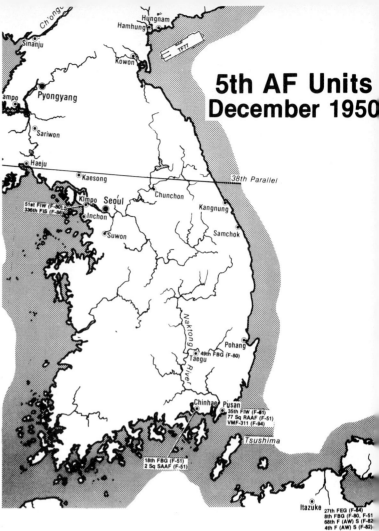

5th AF Units December 1950

Capt. Morris Pitts' "Punkin-head" crashed at K-13 when experimental, high explosive .50 calibre ammo blew up in the right gunbay, taking out the flight hydraulics. (Janney)

Sgt. Billie Beach
12 April 1951, B-29 Gunner, 19BG

reprinted courtesy of Air Force Magazine, published by the Air Force Assn.

It was my 19th mission and the 3rd on the "No Sweat". Our targets were the bridges over the Yalu near Sinuiju, within sight of the *MiG* base at Antung. Twelve B-29s were assigned to the mission, all loaded with 2,000 lb bombs. We were to get fighter cover from *F-84s* and *F-86s* before entering *MiG* Alley.

We took off at dawn into a bright clear day - perfect for flying. About 40 minutes out we test-fired our guns and then settled down for a long ride. Two hours later we started to climb to our assigned altitude and leveled off. A few minutes later, we picked up our fighter cover.

About noon we were alerted that we were approaching the target area. We were less than five minutes away from the bridges - and the *MiGs*. Suddenly the tail gunner shouted into his mike: "*MiGs*, about 30 of 'em, coming in at 6 o'clock!" They were *MiGs* alright, coming in fast at 6 o'clock and breaking away at four - right in line with my sights. I watched as they shot at the tail first then swung to hit us amidship.

They were coming so close that I could see the muzzle-blast from their 23mm cannon. I started firing as soon as I got one in range. I caught my first *MiG* on his breakaway. I tracked him and kept firing short bursts until he went out of control about 900 yards out. He went straight down, spinning like crazy.

Three minutes and four passes later, I spied this other guy coming in low at 1:30. I picked him up about 1200 yards out and chopped into him with short steady bursts. That *MiG* got out about 400 yards, keeled over on its side and went into a headlong dive. I watched it crash and explode on the mountainside. That was my last shot at the *MiGs* as the fighters moved in on them.

But they'd hurt the "No Sweat" plenty bad. Number 2 and 4 engines were shot out and feathered. The right aileron was shot out. The interphone was out and No. 2 fuel tank caught fire. Our formation was broken up as two of the four aircraft had been shot down. The third ship had to turn back for Okinawa, so we were all alone.

The AC rang the alert bell to prepare to bail out and all of a sudden I got scared. I'd never jumped before and I didn't want to start now. The Commies were throwing flak up at us now. I could see the little black puffs all along the wings and engines. But the bailout signal never came and it dawned on

us that we were going to try to make the bomb run anyway.

The AC tried to catch the flight up ahead of us but with two engines out it was impossible. So we went it alone. It seemed we were suspended in space. Like a bird with a broken wing, we limped in over the bridges. When we left, we could see that the bridges were gone.

The next hour was the longest of my young life. We lost altitude and the AC had to depressurize the cabin. It got so cold we nearly froze. Each minute we dropped closer to the mountains. It was the most spectacular flying I've ever seen. We were just barely in the air when we broke out over an advanced fighter base near the Han River. The runway was way too short but we went in anyway. When we touched down the main gear collapsed and we slid in on the belly and nose wheel. The old "No Sweat" came to a halt with her nose over the road near the strip. it was 1400 and she disrupted traffic.

Flying again from Suwon, the *F-86s* could reach *MiG* Alley. LtCol. Bruce Hinton's "Squanee" shows off the black/white ID stripes used by the 4th FIG. (Campbell)

1000 lb. bombs being loaded on "All Shook". *MiGs* made life miserable for *B-29* crews trying to bomb in *MiG* Alley. (USAF)

20 May 1951 and Capt. James Jabara gets a victory ride after shooting down two more *MiGs* to become the first all-jet ace in history. (USAF)

Although the *MiGs* did get a few *B-29s*, all *B-29* objectives were achieved in May, with the exception of one bridge at Sinuiju which just wouldn't drop. May also saw the first ace of the Korean War crowned when Capt. James Jabara got No. 5 and 6 on the 20th.

Capt. James Jabara
20 May 1951, 334th FIS, F-86A
No. 49-1318

I'd begun to think that I never was going to get a chance at that 5th *MiG*. It had been almost a month since I got my 4th and the *MiGs* hadn't been in a fighting mood. I was in the second batch of *Sabres* on a fighter sweep down the Yalu. As we were climbing to altitude, we could hear the first flights chattering over the RT. They had been jumped by a big gaggle of *MiGs*, about 50, and they were calling for us to hurry up.

We climbed to 35,000 feet and promptly dropped tanks, all except me. One of my tanks just wouldn't come off. Orders were that if you had a 'hung tank', you were to beat it for home. But I wasn't about to lose what may be my last shot at becoming an ace. I called Kemp, my wingman, and told him that we were joining the fight.

The airplane was very stiff flying with one tank, but we found about a half dozen *MiGs* coming in on us. Another pair of *Sabres* split the *MiG* formation and we tacked onto the other three. I was just setting up for a firing position when three more *MiGs* attacked us.

They overshot me as I turned into them. Two broke away but I latched onto the tail of the third one. He tried everything in the book to shake me but he couldn't. I closed to within

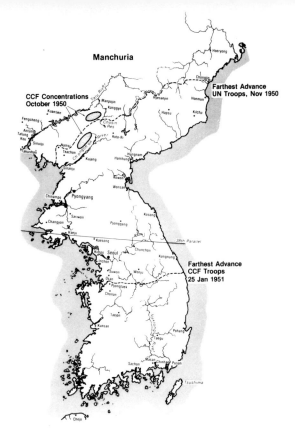

Advance of the CCF

1500 feet and gave him three good bursts. I saw the APIs hit his fuselage and left wing. He did two violent snap rolls and started to spin. At 10,000 feet, with Kemp and I circling him, the *MiG* pilot bailed out. It was a good thing for him that he didn't wait any longer because the *MiG* exploded a few seconds later. With Kemp covering me, I shot some gun camera film of the explosion.

The next few minutes were wild with 28 *Sabres* trying to watch some 50 *MiGs* buzzing around them like angry bees. I climbed back up to 20,000 feet and spotted six more *MiGs*. I was in a good position so I bounced them. Picking one of them out, I closed the range and got off two good bursts, scoring heavily both times on his fuselage and tail surfaces. he flamed out right away with smoke pouring from his exhaust. One more burst caught him right in the middle and he caught fire.

Quickly I cut my power and popped the speed brakes, following him down to about 6500 feet to make sure he hit the ground. All of a sudden I heard a popcorn machine right in my cockpit. Looking back, I saw two *MiGs* firing at me. And they had very good position. Kemp should have warned me but he had been busy with some other *MiGs* while I was attacking these. I was in big trouble!

Breaking left, I went to full throttle and closed the brakes. For about two minutes we went all over the sky with them shooting all the time and me running like hell, and doing some jinks and things that the *F-86* wasn't meant to do. Then I heard two other guys from my flight on the RT "There's an *F-86* in trouble down there!" I came right on with "Roger, I know it only too damned well!" "Call us if you need help!" they said. Since I was on 'Bingo Fuel' I said "I sure could use some!"

The two *F-86s* rolled over and came down to my aid. They were just beautiful! One *MiG*, seeing help on the way, broke off and ran for home. The other *MiG* held on and kept firing. Gene Holley was one of the *F-86* drivers. He pulled in behind the *MiG* and started to pour fire into him. We flew round and round. Me running, the *MiG* firing at me, Holley firing at him, and Pitts, in the other *86,* covering all of us. The *MiG* soon started to smoke and broke off his attack and headed back across the Yalu. Since we were all well below 'bingo', none of us could give chase. I called Holley "Thanks for saving my neck!" It had been a very rough 20 minutes.

No. 2 Sq., SAAF, flew its first combat mission in December 1950. The 'Springboks' flew *F-51s* with the 18th FBG until conversion to *F-86Fs* in Spring 1953. (USAF via Garrett)

A 3rd BG *B-26* attacking Chinese concentrations near the MLR in Spring 1951. With 18 forward firing machine guns, the *B-26* was a very formidable anti-personnel weapon. (USAF)

"Brown Nose" flew the 10,000th sortie for the 452nd BG(L). (USAF)

When this *C-119* crashed at Pusan East, the 35th FIW crews promptly converted it into a snack bar, complete with kitchen. (USAF)

RB-45Cs from the 91st SRS flew the dangerous Yalu River recon missions. The first inflight refueling of a combat aircraft involving a 91st *RB-45* and a 91st *KB-29*, took place on 14 July 1951. (USAF)

334th FIS *F-86As* on line at K-13. "Nosey Rosie" was Capt. J. L. Brooks' aircraft, the first pilot to chase a *MiG* across the Yalu. (Australian War Memorial)

LtCol. Glen Eagleston added 3 *MiGs* to his 18½ WWII victories. Note tiny squadron emblem under windscreen. Winged star is blue with red 'wing'. Kills were not carried at this time. (Australian War Memorial)

June 1951 saw the introduction of the Reds' "Big Team" and "Little Team" to combat. It was quite evident that the 'Big Team' was made up of the Russian instructor pilots. A fight with the 'Big Team' on 17 June saw 1 *MiG* destroyed and 6 damaged - no *Sabre* losses. On 18 June *MiGs* jumped 32 *Sabres* - 5 *MiGs* confirmed to one *Sabre* lost. Again on 19 June - 4 *MiGs* destroyed to one *Sabre*. The 'Little Team' was the *Po-2s*, Bedcheck Charlies, that slipped in under the radar. The 'Little Team' lost their first one when he happened to find himself in front of a returning *B-26* near Suwon. You'd be amazed what 14 .50 calibres can do to a fabric airplane!

In July, the *MiGs* penetrated as far south as PyongYang. And these *MiG* drivers were quite good, using new tactics such as the 'Yo-Yo'. The 'Yo-Yo' started as a Lufberry of *MiGs* about 5,000 feet above the *Sabres*. Single *MiGs* then dove down in a transonic firing pass and then zoom-climb up to another Lufberry. It was effective until the *Sabres* started spiraling down to a lower altitude where *MiG* performance dropped off. Another new one was the 'Zoom and Sun' in which the *MiGs* just waited in the sun about 48,000 feet. When the *F-86s* appeared, they'd simply dive down on them, make a run, and then climb back to altitude. Both took advantage of the much greater rate of climb that the *MiGs* possessed.

But no matter who was flying the *MiGs*, or what tactics they used, the *MiG* drivers never seemed to learn that they simply couldn't stay with the big wing fighter-bombers like the F-51, F-80 and F4U at low altitudes. The older prop planes could simply turn away from the *MiG*, cut the throttle and the *MiG* would be looking at empty sky. LtCol. Kendall Carlson shot down a *MiG* in November 1950 and Flt.Lt.Peter Carmichael got one in a Royal Navy *Sea Fury* from *HMS Ocean* on 9 August 1952. Capt. Jesse Folmar from VMF-312 tells how he got one in an *F4U Corsair* on 10 September .

We were flying from the *Sicily* on an interdiction mission over North Korea when 4 *MiG 15s* jumped us. They attacked in pairs. The second section had just passed and was in a climbing left turn. I turned inside them and gave the nearest one a five second burst of 20mm. The *MiG* belched black smoke and the pilot ejected. His chute opened, but it was already on fire.

The war in Korea saw the first use of the so-called 'smart bomb'. In the Autumn of 1950, B-29s started dropping 1,000lb Razon bombs. The Razon, developed during WWII, had radio controlled tail fins which the bombardier controlled. After some initial problems, they proved highly accurate but weren't powerful enough to knock out bridges. Usually 4 bombs were required to knock out one span. The Razon was replaced with the 12,000lb Tarzon bomb. This one could take out a bridge, 2 spans at a time, with one hit. It was the beginning of a new era in tactical bombing.

RF-80A of the 45th TRS in the snow at K-14. The 45th was part of the 67th TRW which was charged with all the tactical recon work in Korea. (USAF)

"Tulie, Scotty & ?", an RF-51D with the 45th TRS. Spinner, wing and stab tips are blue with white dots. Tail tip is yellow. (Picciani Aircraft Slide)

The Royal Australian Air Force's No. 77 Sq. traded their F-51s for new Meteor Mk 8s in July 1951. They were no match for the MiGs. (Hendle}

Operation Strangle saw maximum use of every aircraft. Here is an 8th FBW *F-80C* leaving K-13 with 4 1000lb bombs. (USAF)

18th FBG and No. 2 Sq., SAAF *F-51s* used many HVAR rockets in both close support and ResCAP missions. (USAF via Garrett)

Interdiction was the prime mission of all UN aircraft. In May 1951 Operation Strangle was begun. Designed to paralyze the Red lines of supply north of the 38th Parallel, it was initially successful. But when the 8th Army stopped advancing, the Reds were allowed to resupply at their leisure.

Overall, the Reds had suffered such a beating that in early 1951 there was a noticeable reduction in air activity until the first Russian "volunteers" showed up in June. As a smokescreen, the Russian UN Delegate suggested that the Korean problem be solved by negotiation. In July 1951, Radio Peking asked that truce talks be started at Kaesong. The talks began but they had little effect on FEAF operations.

FEAF used the temporary slowdown in combat operations in Spring 1951 to rebuild its facilities. Kimpo was repaired and Suwon had its runway extended, and parking ramps and taxiways laid down. A brand new airfield was built at Kunsan and the PSP runway at Taegu, which had totally collapsed in May, was replaced with a concrete one. With Kimpo's runways back in shape in June, the F-80s of the 8th FBW moved in. But they found that the runway was too short for a fully armed F-80. So, in late August when Suwon had its extended runway finished, the 8th traded bases with the 4th FIW. Kimpo would be the home of the 4th, the

Meteor jets of No. 77 Sq RAAF, and the 67th TRG.

While the truce talks brought most of the ground fighting to a halt, the air battles on the Yalu continued to rage. The 4th FIW got two more aces in September when 1Lt. Richard Becker and Capt. Ralph "Hoot" Gibson each got their 5th. This was due to the fact that the Reds were making a full effort at gaining air superiority over *MiG* Alley. Outnumbering the *Sabres* up to 6-1, they entered *MiG* Alley in groups of up to 100 aircraft. Using every tactic in the book, including head-on passes like Luftwaffe pilots did on *B-17s*, sheer numbers began to have an effect. FEAF had to pull its fighter-bombers out of operations in *MiG* Alley.

No sooner was this done than the Reds began putting jet fighter bases inside North Korea again. Saamcham, Taechon, Uiju, all started building bases capable of taking the *MiG 15*. FEAF countered by increasing the *Sabre* patrols over the Yalu, thus attempting to cut the *MiG* force down to size. Then B-29s started hitting the new Red bases. First night radar-bombing was tried. It worked but was slow. Finally, the decision was made to send the *29s* back into *MiG* Alley in daylight. The first mission to Saamcham caught the Reds by surprise. No *MiGs* came up to challenge the big bombers.

October 1951 saw the first *F-86Es* arrive in Korea. The *Es* first went to the 51st FIW at K-13, who traded in their *F-80Cs*. (NAA)

But the *MiGs* came up on 22 October over Taechon. One *B-29* was lost. On 23 October, the *MiGs* were waiting for the *29s* over Namsi. 100 *MiGs* jumped all over the 34 *F-86s* screening for the *29s*. With the *F-86s* thus contained, 50 *MiGs* hit the *B-29* force with brutal attacks. The *F-84s* that were escorting were completely outclassed. When it was all over, 3 *B-29s* went down along with 1 *F-84*. The *B-29* force had suffered major damage to ALL aircraft. FEAF decided that the *B-29s* could no longer operate in daylight hours. The *MiGs* had finally won a battle.

The air battle at Namsi was the deciding factor in the USAF decision to re-equip the 51st FIW with *Sabres*. 75 brand-new *F-86Es* were loaded on the jeep carriers **Cape Esperance** and **Sitko Bay** and sent to Japan. Since the 51st had only two squadrons, the 16th and 25th, the 4th FIW also got some of the new E models.

The MiGs were trying out more new tactics on the *F-86s*. 'Bandit Trains' of around 75 *MiGs* would cross the Yalu at points about 40 miles apart. Flying at 40,000 feet, and dropping off flights to engage the *Sabre* patrols, the main body would fly south with both 'trains' meeting over PyongYang. Swinging back north, now with some 120 *MiGs*, they would jump any UN aircraft in the area. Another 'train' would come across the river to cover the first two on withdrawal. The fuel starved *Sabres*, bound for home after fighting the *MiGs* on the Yalu, were to be caught in this pincers. Had the Red pilots been well trained or aggressive, the results could have been disastrous.

November and December 1951 saw more aces crowned as Major Richard Creighton got his 5th *MiG* on 27 November. 30 November was a very bad day for the Red air commanders. As they attempted to move 16 *La-9s* and 12 *Tu-2* bombers into the new base at Taehwa-do, 31 *Sabres* caught up with the force. First they split the *MiG* top cover and then went in for the kill on the slower propeller planes. It was a slaughter, the final tally being 8 *Tu-2s*, 3 *La-9s*, and 1 *MiG* destroyed. Major George Davis got 3 of the *Tu-2s* and the lone *MiG* himself, making him the 5th ace in Korea. Major Winton Marshall got a *Tu-2* and a *La-9* to become Ace No. 6.

The 51st FIW flew their first *F-86* combat sorties on 1 December. They were led by Col. Francis "Gabby" Gabreski of WWII *P-47* fame. He came over from the 4th along with a cadre of some of the best pilots in the 4th. It wasn't long before the 51st started knocking *MiGs* out of the sky, getting their first *MiG* on 2 December.

On 13 December the Reds put up a big effort with 145 *MiGs* meeting the *Sabres*. They were met head-on, 13 *MiGs* going down. Major Davis got four of them alone making him the first all-jet double ace in history. After this day, the *MiGs* came in very high and made very few aggressive moves.

The first missions flown were training missions with 4th Wing pilots leading. 51st was the first unit to use the yellow and black ID stripes, at this time a Wing ID marking. (NAA)

Training and combat orientation flights later were flown in *T-33s* such as "Miss Marlene". Nose and tank flashes in red, edged black. Tail checks are black on silver. (Chapman)

The 4th Wing also got *Es* but still retained a large number of *F-86As*. 272 is an *A* model while 769, "Bernie's Bo", is an *E*. (USAF)

It was at this time that the *Sabre* pilots began to note a definite pattern in *MiG* flight tactics. It was much like that used in a training class. First the *MiG* 'class' would fly very high and fast, avoiding combat. Over a period of weeks, they'd start to come down in altitude and some of them would attempt to engage the *Sabres*. Finally, after a few months, they would fight very willingly to see how good they had become. If they survived the 'graduation', they rotated out and a new 'class' was brought in, with the cycle repeating. This was very frustrating for the *F-86* drivers who wanted nothing more than to mix it up with the *MiGs*. Even though the *MiGs* entered the 'Alley' in formations of up to 200 planes, they'd sit at about 48,000 feet, 'right on the mach', and cruise back and forth. The *Sabres*, even the 51st Wing's new E models, simply couldn't get to them.

On both 6 and 25 January, the 51st went all the way to 45,000 feet and caught some of the *MiGs* by surprise. Some of the *MiGs* were at their altitudes and the 51st pilots shot 25 of them down. In the same month, the 4th Wing flying a mixed bag of *F-86As* and *Es* got only 5 confirmed, pointing up the need to replace the old A models.

Another problem arose for the *Sabres* - maintenance. When the 51st Wing got its *Sabres*, it put the FEAF logistics people in one hell of a bind. They had barely enough equipment to support one *Sabre* wing. Now there were twice the aircraft with twice the problems. In January 1952, maintenance and parts problems kept 45% of all *Sabres* grounded. Drop tanks were in such short supply that ¡*Sabres* often went on patrol with only one tank. It became routine to see the *Sabres* return from the Yalu and make dead-stick landings, completely out of fuel. The parts situation wasn't remedied until Col. Harry Thyng, CO of the 4th, sent a TWX direct to General Vandenberg, Air Force Chief of Staff, over all the heads at Fifth Air Force and FEAF. He explained the problems he had getting *F-86* parts and replacements. Chiefs of Staff have a way of getting things done and by March the *F-86* parts crisis was resolved.

February saw a *MiG* 'class' go into finals week and they came to fight.

Col. Ben Preston congratulates Majors George Davis and Winton Marshall for the kills that made both of them aces on 30 November 1951.

Col. Gabreski in front of the "Lady Frances". He and Bill Wescott both made ace in the "Lady". (Collins)

"Mach Knocker" illustrates the early markings carried by the 51st FIW *Sabres* - a blue scroll carrying the names of the pilot and ground crew. Blue is the 16th FIS color. Nose of the aircraft is natural fibreglass brown, not red. (USAF)

Maj. William Whisner
20 February 1952, 25 FIS, F-86E No. 51-2735

By the day of the mission when the shared victory occurred, both Gabby (Col. Gabreski) and I had been credited with 4 *MiGs* each. Another kill for either of us would make one of us the 7th ace of the Korean War. On this mission, both Gabby and I were leading different flights. Gabby and his bunch, as usual, found a bunch of *MiGs*. From a distance, I saw the fight spiral down through the contrail level and I set up a cut-off vector on the gaggle. Shortly, I picked up 6 *MiGs,* in string, being chased by 4 *F-86s.* As I pulled in close behind the No. 4 F-86 with my wingman, I identified the flight as Gabby's.

Gabby was firing at the last *MiG* and shortly lit him up with APIs. The *MiG* began to smoke but didn't slow down, continuing due north away from us. At this point, the Yalu River was under our nose and Gabby's wingman called that we were crossing the river. I immediately transmitted to Gab and said "Stay with the *MiG*, he's got to go down!" However, Gabby broke off with the *MiG* still smoking north, hell for leather. After Gab's flight broke off, I stayed with the *MiG* and he flew north for about 25 or 30 miles. I only stayed with him to confirm the victory for Gabreski. The *MiG* still had not slowed any, but was apparently low on fuel as he began to dip his left wing as though to see whether I was still behind him. Finally, about 50 miles into Manchuria, he turned sharp

Maintenance was a critical problem for the *Sabres* until Col. Harrison Thyng took the problem direct to the Chief of Staff. "Minimum Effort" is shown undergoing an engine change. (USAF)

left. I knew then, with my aircraft on 'Bingo' fuel, that I had to hit him to finish him off.

I fired, observed a few API hits on his fuselage, and he blew his canopy and bailed out.

Returning to base, I ascertained that Gabby had already claimed a 'probable', then filed a mission report confirming the claim as 'destroyed' for Gabreski, not mentioning that I had hit the *MiG*. However, that evening my room phone rang and it was Gabby. He asked me whether I had fired at and hit the *MiG*. He then ordered me not to lie as he would get the truth from my wingman. I then relented and admitted that I had hit the *MiG* but said it was no matter as it was a gone goose anyhow. Gabby disagreed and ordered me to change my mission report. I respectfully declined. He became angered and demanded that I do as he said. Again I declined. He then slammed the receiver down in my ear. About 10 minutes later, the phone rang again and a calmer Gabreski told me that we would share the *MiG*. Both Gabby and I would have 4½ *MiGs* to our credit. A week or so later, I downed another *MiG* off the tail of Major Don Adams, later to become the 14th ace in Korea. I was the 7th ace in the Korean War. Two months later, Col. Francis Gabreski would become the 8th ace.

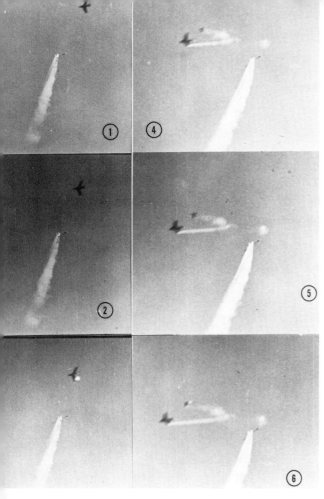

MiG cannon could make large holes in the F-86s as the tail of FU-227 illustrates. (Moore via Menard)

(Above) A series of photos showing both a MiG and a Sabre being shot down. The MiG is already smoking in No. 1. In No. 3 he hits the Sabre in the left wing, blowing it off in No. 4. In No. 6 the Sabre is out of control and the MiG is smoking badly. (USAF)

(Below) This F-84E from the 136th FBS caught fire after an emergency landing at K-2. Flak and MiGs played havoc with USAF fighter-bombers. (Stranberg via Garrett)

(Miller)

When FEAF put *MiG* Alley 'off limits' to everything but *Sabres*, the Reds took advantage and moved *MiGs* into North Korean airfields. This is Uiju with *MiGs* in the revetments. (USAF)

"Command Decision" was the first *B-29* to achieve 'Ace' status. She flew with the 28th BS. (AFM)

Uiju after the *B-29* raids in November 1951. *B-29s* cratered the runways but it was very costly as Bomber Command lost 5 *B-29s*, 2 *F-84s*, 7 *F-86s*, and an *RF-80*. (AFM)

B-29 Squadron Markings

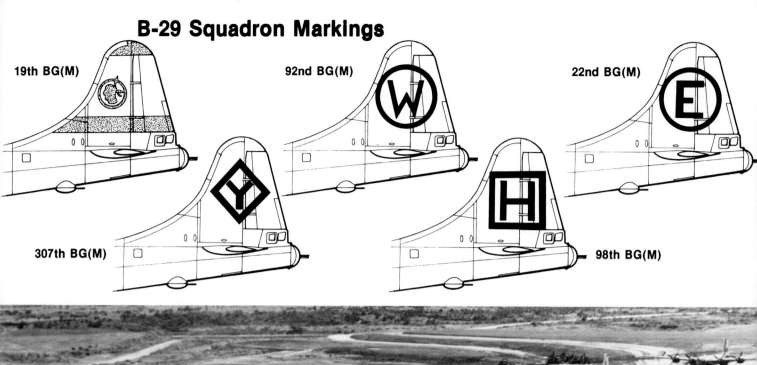

19th BG(M)

307th BG(M)

92nd BG(M)

98th BG(M)

22nd BG(M)

(Above) 19th BG *B-29s* taxiing for takeoff at Kadena AFB, Okinawa. By November 1951, *B-29s* were used only in night attacks. (USAF)

(Below) "Heavenly Laden" from the 98th BG. Nose art was very prevalent on *B-29s.* (USAF)

But February was also a sad month because Major George Davis was shot down. He was leading a flight of four flying cover for some fighter-bombers. His element leader had to retire due to an oxygen problem but Major Davis and his wingman continued the flight. Sighting a dozen *MiGs* trying to intercept the fighter-bombers, Major Davis attacked the superior *MiG* formation. He shot one *MiG* down almost immediately. Although under intense fire from the rear, Major Davis pulled in behind another *MiG*, fired another burst, and the *MiG* burst into flames and went into a vertical dive into the ground. As he was shooting down the third *MiG 15*, his own aircraft suffered a fatal hit and went out of control. Major Davis' aircraft crashed about 30 miles south of the Yalu. For this action, Major Davis was posthumously awarded the Congressional Medal of Honor.

In March, a bunch of *MiG* 'classes' graduated. Most of the *MiGs* stayed up high but a few flights would dive down and mix it up with the *Sabres*. They'd dive, make a firing pass, and then run like hell for the safety of the Yalu river.

In April 1952, no less than five aces were crowned; Col. Gabreski on the 1st, Capt. Robt. Moore on the 3rd, Capt. Iven Kinchloe on the 6th, Capt. Robt. Love on the 21st, and Major Wm. Wescott on the 26th. Major Wescott was the first ace from the 51st Wing to down all his *MiGs* while in the 51st. Gabreski and Whisner both had kills before transferring to the 51st.

May was a slower month for *Sabre* victories. The *MiGs* just didn't come down to fight that often. But they did engage often enough to make four new aces. Capt. Robt. Latshaw and Major Don Adams both got their 5th on 3 May, Lt. James Kasler got his on the 15th, and Col. Harrison Thyng got one to make ace on the 20th. In May, the *Sabre* pilots noticed, to their dismay, that only the best *MiG* pilots seemed to be coming across the Yalu to fight and for the first time, they were being vectored in by GCI (Ground Control Intercept) radar. Several times the *MiGs* would drop out of a heavy cloud cover, right on top of the *Sabres*. The new GCI radars were also used to help the *MiGs* bounce unsuspecting fighter-bombers in the *MiG* Alley area. Between the GCIs and the more proficient *MiG* pilots, the few combats that did occur were costly to FEAF. One *F-51* was lost, three *F-84s* and five *F-86s*. 27 *MiGs* were shot down.

Only on rare occasions did the FEAF pilots have serious trouble countering a *MiG* threat. But try as they might, FEAF could find no solution to the "Bedcheck Charlie" problem. Flying very low and slow, under the FEAF radars, the *Po-2s* would come in almost every night and drop grenades, mortar shells, even some small bombs on the bases. Normally, very little damage was caused. Their main problem was that the pilot's badly needed sleep was being continually disturbed. All types of aircraft were tried — F-82s, F7F-5N Tigercats, even some armed AT-6s.

To help with the "Bedcheck Charlie" problem, USAF committed some Lockheed F-94B Starfires. The 68th FIS sent some of its brand new F-94s to Suwon for strip alert in December 1951. In Spring 1952, the entire 319th FIS was transferred from McChord AFB to Suwon. They flew their first combat mission on 22 March.

The F-94 was big, well armed, fast enough to tangle with the *MiGs*, but unfortunately, not slow enough to handle the Po-2s. One night when a *Po-2* appeared, an F-94 was scrambled. He picked up the Po-2 on his radar but his closure rate was too fast and he flew right through the little biplane, causing both aircraft to crash. Another F-94 tried throttling back with flaps and gear down to stay behind a Po-2. The big F-94 promptly stalled and crashed. The F-94s couldn't do the job.

The Marines tried a few aircraft such as the F7Fs and some night-fighter *Corsairs*. They also moved a brand new aircraft into Korea with the express purpose of stopping "Bedcheck Charlie" - the F3D *Skyknight*. But the best solution was the venerable old *Corsair*. It could fly slow enough, and still maintain control to stay with the Po-2s. This combination would ultimately yield the only Navy ace in Korea - Lt. Guy Bordelon, who got 5 night kills in June/July 1953. The F3Ds were very good at getting the night-fighter *MiGs* which had begun to appear late in 1952.

Pilot - Capt. Oliver Davis, USMC; Radar Operator - WO Dramus Fessler 8 November 1952, F3D-2 Skyknight.

During the night of 8 November, I was assigned the Night Combat Air Patrol (NightCAP) mission, working with

First *F-94Bs* in Korea were from the 68th FIS, who had traded in their *F-82s* in Spring 1951. (USAF)

Fithian's F-94 being rearmed at Suwon. (USAF)

Capt. Ben Fithian points to the star on his *F-94B* representing the first *F-94* kill. (USAF)

Marines flew many types of aircraft trying to check 'Bedcheck Charlie's' activities. These *F4U-5NLs* belong to VMF(N)-513. (Garrett)

Marine Night-Fighter Kills

Capt. Edwin Long	VMF(N)-513	F7F-3N	1 Po-2	30 June 51
Capt. Donald Fenton	VMF(N)-513	F4U-5NL	1 Po-2	12 July 51
Maj. Eugene Van Grundy	VMF(N)-513	F7F-3N	1 Po-2	23 Sept 51
Lt. John Andre	VMF(N)-513	F4U-5NL	1 Yak-9	7 June 52
Maj. Wm. Stratton Jr.	VMF(N)-513	F3D-2	1 Yak-15	3 Nov 52
Capt. Oliver Davis	VMF(N)-513	F3D-2	1 MiG 15	8 Nov 52
Lt. Joseph Corvi	VMF(N)-513	F3D-2	1 Po-2	10 Dec 52
Maj. Elswin Dunn	VMF(N)-513	F3D-2	1 MiG 15	12 Jan 53
Capt. James Weaver	VMF(N)-513	F3D-2	1 Mig 15	28 Jan 53
LtCol. Robert Conley	VMF(N)-513	F3D-2	1 MiG 15	31 Jan 53
LtCol. Robert Conley	VMF(N)-513	F3D-2	1 MiG 15	March 53

an air controller. Around 0130 I was notified that a bogey was at 12 o'clock, 10 miles, and at 12,500 feet. I began a dive from my 19,000 foot altitude and added full power at 14,000 feet. My RO got the contact and ordered me to go "gentle starboard". The contact was lost immediately and I requested further help from the ground controller.

He gave me a heading and repeated that the bogey was still at 12,500 feet. My RO re-established contact with the bogey at 12 o'clock. Again he ordered a gentle starboard turn and I executed a 30 degree bank. We began closing at an indicated air speed of 450 knots. My RO placed us in a position so that the bogey was ten degrees starboard at 12,000 feet. As we closed on him, I got a visual and a jet exhaust. I requested that the ground controller identify the bogey as friend or foe. He replied, "Bag it! Bag it!"

By then I was from a quarter to a half mile from the

The *F3D-2N* of LtCol. R.F. Conley, who shot down 2 night-fighter *MiGs* in early 1953, while he was CO of VMF(N)-513. (Garrett)

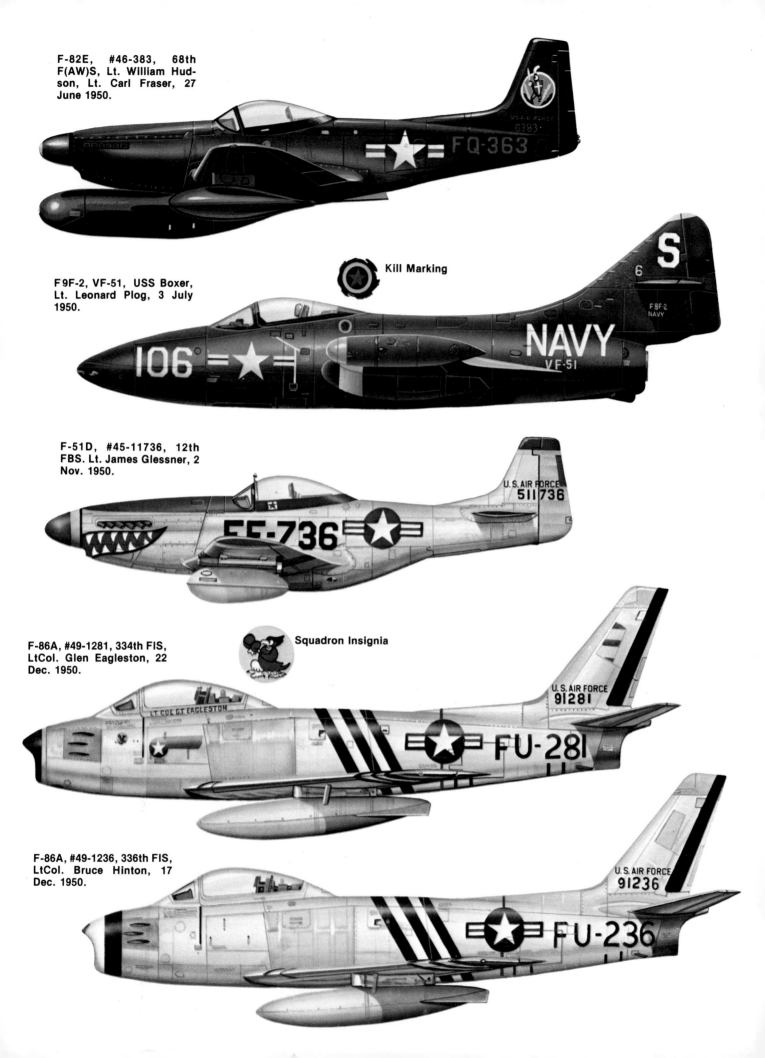

F-82E, #46-383, 68th F(AW)S, Lt. William Hudson, Lt. Carl Fraser, 27 June 1950.

F9F-2, VF-51, USS Boxer, Lt. Leonard Plog, 3 July 1950.

Kill Marking

F-51D, #45-11736, 12th FBS. Lt. James Glessner, 2 Nov. 1950.

F-86A, #49-1281, 334th FIS, LtCol. Glen Eagleston, 22 Dec. 1950.

Squadron Insignia

F-86A, #49-1236, 336th FIS, LtCol. Bruce Hinton, 17 Dec. 1950.

exhaust and closing rapidly. I momentarily popped my speed brakes. The exhaust was so bright it was hard for me to make out the airframe outline. The bandit began a hard turn to starboard. I turned with him and fired a short burst of about 20 rounds from my 20 mm cannon. The 20mm HEI hit in the tailpipe area. There was an explosion and parts flew past my aircraft. I was closing dangerously and pulled hard back on the stick. Since I was already in a hard starboard turn, I passed the bandit to his right.

I observed flames and black smoke coming from the center portion of his aircraft. After reversing my turn, I picked up a visual on the flaming craft as it descended and crashed. There was another explosion upon impact. I had opened fire at 0136 and the bandit crashed at 0137.

During the months of November through July 1952, bridgebusting

became the typical mission. Every railway and highway bridge in North Korea was hit either by FEAF or NavFE aircraft. During the day, the fighter-bombers would work, and at night the B-29s and B-26s went in. "Operation Saturate", the round-the-clock rail interdiction plan, replaced "Operation Strangle" on 22 February 1952. The B-29s were using SHORAN (Short Range Navigation) radar to make their night attacks successful. SHORAN was, quite simply, two ground radar sites telling an airborne bombardier when to bomb. It was not only accurate but it kept the MiG threat down to a minimum.

By the middle of 1952, FEAF had three F-84 wings flying combat missions - the 136thFBG which had replaced the 27th FEW, the 116th FBG and the 49th FBW, which had traded its F-80s for F-84s in the Spring of 1952. It was these units that bore the brunt of the rail-busting missions. On a typical mission, they would be armed with two 1,000lb bombs. They would fly north to the target, for example the rail line between Sinanju and Chongju, drop 400 to 500 bombs on the tracks and go home. But damage would be repaired in a few days. Then the F-84s would have to

First F-84 to garner 1,000 hours of combat time was the "Miss Jacque II" from the 136th FBG. (USAF)

"Operation Strangle" saw the destruction of most of the North Korean rail system. Note the wrecked T-34 tank still on the flatcar. (AFM)

North Korean Railroads

Navy *Corsairs* from VF-884, off the USS Boxer, flew many rail strikes as a part of "Operation Strangle". (US Navy)

"Linda Charlotte" had over 130 missions and was the 49th FBG CO's aircraft. Stripes are red, yellow, blue from nose and tail tip down. (USAF)

"I've been working on the railroad!" (AFM)

go back again. It was a never-ending cycle.

In the months from May through July 1952, these missions brought a new wrinkle to tactical air warfare - inflight refueling of combat loaded fighters. Inflight refueling was not new to the Korean War as *RB-45Cs* from the 91st SRS had been refueling inflight from *KB-29s* from the 91st ARS since July 1951. "Project High Tide" was put into operation on 29 May when 12 *F-84Es* of the 159th FBS/116th FBW refueled in air from *KB-29s* from the 91st ARS after bombing the airfield at Sariwon. On 7 June, the *F-84s* rendezvoused with the tankers over Tsushima before again going to Sariwon. A third IFR mission went to Haeju. The last mission of "Project High Tide" went to PyongYang, refueling both inbound and out over Miho. The project was a huge success with only bad weather hampering any of the missions.

June 1952 saw airpower being used as a political weapon for the first time. When the peace talks stalled, FEAF was ordered to 'jolt' the Reds back to the peace table. An electrical jolt! The North Korean hydroelectric plants would be attacked for the first time. The toughest would go first - Suiho. This was easily the roughest target as the area had 44 heavy and 37 light anti-aircraft guns. Add to this the fact that it was only four minutes

from Antung where some 300 to 400 *MiGs* lay in wait.

On 23 June, at 1600 hrs. a combined FEAF and NavFE effort was launched on the power plants. With 84 *Sabres* flying top cover, 35 Navy *Skyraiders*, 35 *Panthers*, 79 *F-84s*, and 45 *F-80s* dropped 145 tons of bombs on Suiho. At the same time *F-51s* hit Fusen, Marine *Corsairs* struck Chosin, and *Panthers*, *Corsairs* and *Skyraiders* hit the other Fusen plants. After four days, and 1276 sorties, 90% of North Korean power potential was gone. A complete blackout was in effect for over two weeks. It caused major setbacks in the military industries in northeast China and Manchuria. The cost was two Navy planes, both pilots being rescued.

June also saw the crowning of another 5th AF ace, Lt. James Low - only 6 months out of flight school! In July, the 51st Wing got a third squadron, the 39th FIS. The 51st and 4th FIWs started receiving the new *F-86F Sabre*. The *E* model had closed the gap between *MiG* and *Sabre* performance, giving the *F-86* much better control in the transonic speed ranges. Now the *F* brought a more powerful engine resulting in higher top speeds and more altitude. Finally, the *Sabres* would be able to go UP to the *MiGs* and get them! July also saw two of the *F-84* units transferred on paper only. The 116th FBG and 136th FBW, both National Guard units,

F-51D, #44-75728, 67th FBS,
Maj. A. "Moon" Mullins,
February 1951.

F-84G, #51-493, 523rd FES,
Lt. Jacob Kratt, January
1951.

U.S. AIR FORCE
493

FS-493-D

Squadron Insignia

INTELLIGENT STRENGTH

F-84E, #51-490, 523rd FES,
LtCol. William Bertram,
January 1951.

U.S. AIR FORCE
490

FS-490-D

"Lady Frances", an F-86E belonging to Maj. William Wescott, who
got 5 kills. Col. Francis Gabreski also flew "Lady Frances".
(Collins)

"Michigan Center/Lady
Frances", F-86E, #51-2746,
25th FIS, Col. Francis Gabreski, 2 Oct. 1951.

LADY
FRANCES

U.S. AIR FORCE
12746

FU-746

MICHIGAN
CENTER

Kill Marks

F9F-2, VF-781, USS Bon
Homme Richard, Lt.JG
J.D. Middleton, 18 Nov.
1951.

D

NAVY
VF-781

114

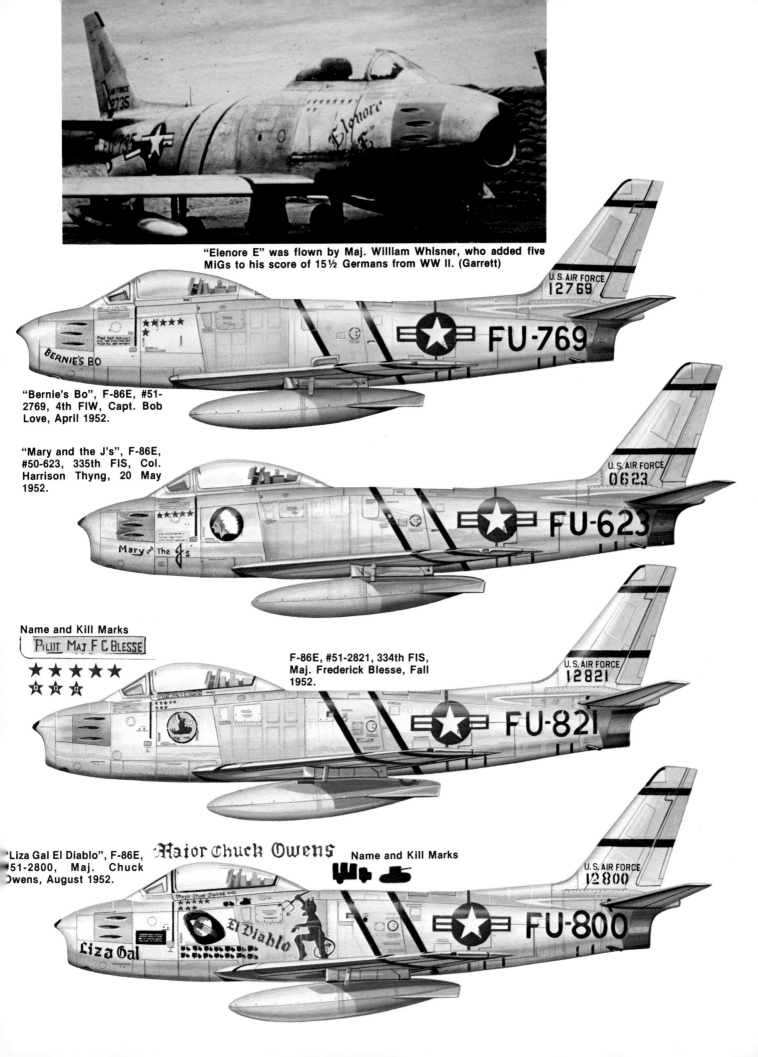

"Elenore E" was flown by Maj. William Whisner, who added five MiGs to his score of 15½ Germans from WW II. (Garrett)

"Bernie's Bo", F-86E, #51-2769, 4th FIW, Capt. Bob Love, April 1952.

"Mary and the J's", F-86E, #50-623, 335th FIS, Col. Harrison Thyng, 20 May 1952.

Name and Kill Marks

PILOT MAJ F C BLESSE

F-86E, #51-2821, 334th FIS, Maj. Frederick Blesse, Fall 1952.

"Liza Gal El Diablo", F-86E, #51-2800, Maj. Chuck Owens, August 1952.

Major Chuck Owens   Name and Kill Marks

(Above) The USS Bon Homme Richard makes ready for takeoff. *ADs* and *Corsairs* will leave before the *Panthers* so that the jets won't waste fuel waiting for the prop aircraft to catch up. (US Navy)

(Below) 8th FBS CO's aircraft taxiing at Taegu, ready to head north. Stripes are yellow and black. (USAF)

were redesignated the 474th and 58th FBG respectively. The personnel and aircraft remained the same although new *F-84Gs* were on the way.

Although the majority of the *MiGs* were staying away from combat throughout the Summer of 1952, the ones that did come to fight were among the better pilots that the Reds had. *Sabre* drivers referred to them as 'Honchos'. Several of them were observed at close enough range, both in and out of the cockpit, to see that they were not Orientals. July saw 19 *MiGs* go down with a loss of 4 *Sabres*. August saw 33 *MiGs* downed, 2 *Sabres* lost, and Capt. Clifford Jolley gained Ace status.

In September FEAF tried to draw the *MiGs* into battle by bombing targets in *MiG* Alley again. The Reds responded with *MiG* sorties for the month totaling 1857. Many major air battles took place during September including one on 4 September in which the *MiGs* kept jumping back and forth across the Yalu to attack the *Sabres*. Seventeen separate air battles took place and in one of them Major Frederick "Boots" Blesse got his 5th *MiG* to become No. 19 on the Ace list. On the 9th, 175 *MiGs* jumped some *Sabres* and *F-84s* that were bombing the NKPA Military Academy at Sakchu. On the 21st, the *MiGs* attempted to break up an *F-84* attack on a munitions plant near Sinuiju. During the fight, Capt. Robinson Risner got his fifth *MiG*.

Formation of *F-84s* from the 474th FBG over North Korea. Note the different tail markings. *F-84* unit markings are very confusing due to the constant shuffling of units and their adoption of each others markings. (USAF)

F-84 Squadron Markings

116th FBG July 51 - 10 July 52
474th FBG 10 July 52 - 1 April 53
49th FBG From 1 April 53

49th FBG Spring 51 - 1 April 53
474th FBG From 1 April 53

58th FBG From 10 July 52

27th FEG Dec 50 - May 51
136th FBG May 51 - 10 July 52

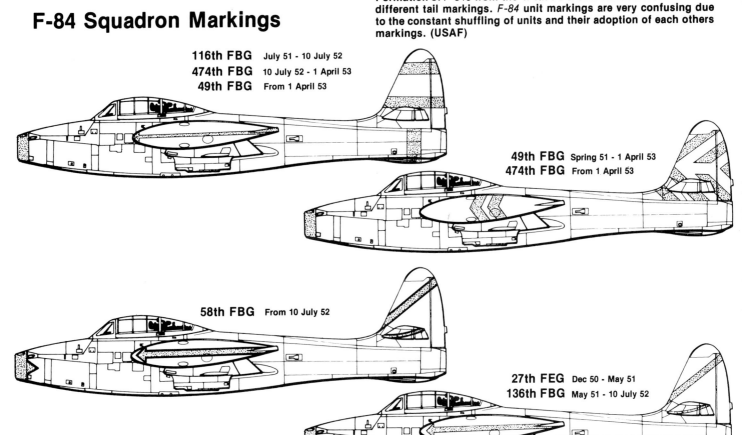

F4U-5N, VMA-312, Capt. Jesse Folmar, 10 Sept. 1952.

Kill Marking

"Honest John", F-86E, #51-2747, 336th FIS, Col. Walker Mahurin, Sept. 1952.

"Hell-er Bust X", F-86E, #51-2756, 16th FIS, LtCol. Ed Heller, 22 Jan. 1953.

Pilot Capt. Cecil G. Foster

Name Plate

"Four Kings & A Queen", F-86E, #51-2738, 16th FIS, Capt. Cecil Foster, 24 Jan. 1953.

F3D-2, VMF(N)-513, LtCol. R. F. Conley, M/Sgt. J.N. Scott, March 1953.

"Patricia" was the mount of 'Jolting' Joe Romack. (Hendle)

"Patricia II", F-86E, #51-2834, 336th FIS, Lt. Joe Romack, Spring 1953.

Col. "King" Baker

Angel Face & The Babes

"Angel Face & The Babes/The King", F-86E, #51-2822, 336th FIS, Col. Royal Baker, Spring 1953.

Opposite Nose

Maj. James Jabara taxies out for a mission. Note that he is flying Capt. Fernandez' aircraft, FU-857. "Jabby" used many aircraft to get his 15 MiGs. (Hendle)

F-86F, #51-2857, 334th FIS, Capt. Manuel Fernandez, May 1953.

MiG in the gunsight of an F-86. Note 'pipper' circle above the MiG. (USAF)

Capt. Robinson Risner
5 August 1952, 336th FIS, F-86E
"John Red Lead"

My flight was on alert and it was almost time for them to be awakened. I waited for about thirty minutes before I roused them. My element leader prevailed on me to take a nap, which I did. Then I went out to the alert pad, took over as flight lead, switched the parachutes and equipment, rigged my airplane, put on my helmet, and laid down on the wing.

I had almost dropped off to sleep when the horn sounded. That particular day we were the hot shot flight. That meant we were "clean" (no wing tanks) and ready for action. We scrambled and went whipping down the runway two at a time. I was still getting my equipment on and closing the canopy on the takeoff roll. On my wing was a kid making his first combat mission. He had a big handlebar moustache, was fresh out of combat training school at Nellis, and was very eager.

Leveling off at 35,000 feet, I saw eight MiGs cross a thousand feet below us, going from left to right, a perfect setup. One high side pass and we would really cream them. I had learned though, that after spotting one formation, always check your six o'clock because they normally had someone watching over them. "Check Six" I called to the flight. Red 3 came back with "Lead, we've got six at 3 o'clock high and starting in!" As they came in firing, two of them overshot. I whipped back over on the tail of one of them at about one thousand feet range.

I laid the bright red circle of the gun sight on the tailpipe of one of them and gave him a good long burst. He lit up like a Christmas tree from the APIs. He had just started to make a right climbing turn when his engine evidently quit. I must have knocked it out, because he seemed to stop in mid-air. I chopped my throttle back to idle and threw my speed brakes

out. I was doing everything I could to stay behind him. As he stalled he fell off on his left wing and started to go into a spin. My aircraft stalled too, and I kicked the left rudder unconsciously. It looked for a second as if my gunsight would fall right through him.

I thought to myself, "This is my first MiG!" I held down the trigger and all six fifties started chugging away. I could smell the powder smoke. I was only three hundred feet from him when I cut his tail off just above the fuselage. The tail went one way and the fuselage spun in the other direction. We were at 32,000 feet. He panicked, bailed out and opened his chute. I imagine he was frozen stiff as a poker by the time he hit the ground.

Major Robinson Risner
4 December 1952, 336th FIS, F-86F
"John Red Lead"

I saw a lot of flying while in Korea, but the best pilot I came across was not an American. We were flying close escort for some fighter-bombers that were trying to knock out a chemical plant near Sinuiju. Normally, we did not cross the Yalu, but on this mission we had to do a 360 turn between the fighter-bombers and the potential MiG threat. The 360 took us right over the Antung Air University.

We hadn't even made one orbit when we met four MiGs head-on. Seeing one another about the same time, both the MiG flight and my flight dropped tanks. The MiGs weren't too eager for a fight and made a 180 degree turn and headed toward Fen Cheng Airfield.

Afraid that if I lost sight of them, they might make a descending turn and come back on the bombers, I stayed with them. They did and my radar gunsight locked onto the tail-end Charlie. Although I was at maximum range, I fired a short burst. I knew that I had hit him in the canopy because the glass began to fly. He made a hard turn into me and the other three made a right descending turn away from me.

I told Red 3 and 4 to go after the other three and I would

When the *MiGs* increased their formation sizes, the *F-86s* did the same. Mass takeoffs at K-13 and 14 were normal after the Summer of 1952. (USAF)

take care of this one since I had already hit him. He came hard into me and I turned inside of him. When I rolled out, I was within 1500 feet of him — I pulled the nose down and gave him another short burst. It sparkled him a little bit. When I did, he did a half roll and hung upside down, then did a complete roll and ended up upside down again.

Meanwhile, we were descending, making about .95 Mach. We were getting real low when he rolled it a second time and started a Split S for the ground. I didn't think he would make it, so I widened my turn slightly to leave a little more room between the ground and me. "Two! This is going to be the easiest kill I ever had!" I just knew he was going to splatter.

But as I watched, he pulled out down a dry river bed! The dust billowed up and he stayed right on the deck. He was so low he was throwing up small rocks. I dropped down to get him, but to hit him I had to get down behind him in his jet wash. There was so much turbulence that I couldn't do anything in it.

This guy was one fantastic pilot. When I did get down in his jet wash, he'd chop the throttle and throw out his speed-brakes, forcing me to overshoot. I would coast up beside him, wingtip to wingtip, and look him right in the eye. When it looked like I was going to overshoot him, I'd pull up, roll over the top and come down on the other side of him. When I did, he'd throw the coal to it and go into a hard turn, pulling all the Gs he could. About the time I'd get the pipper on him, he'd push the stick forward and go into an inverted turn, which is extremely difficult and hard on the eyes and body. I couldn't duplicate that and would roll into an opposite turn and start to catch him again.

One time he actually flipped upside down, went up the side of a small mountain, over the top and pulled it through down the other side. I was right side up, so when I went over the top I had to do a half roll to go down the other side. I was having a real difficult time, but I was hitting him occasionally. I had shot away part of his tail, his canopy was missing, and his left side was afire. He wasn't in very good shape but he was fighting like a cornered rat.

We were down in the river bed again and my wingman was hollering "Hit him Lead! Get him!" Believe me, I was doing my best! The *MiG* pilot chopped the throttle, threw his speed brakes out, I coasted up and was afraid I was going to overshoot him. I rolled over the top again, coming down on the other side just off his wingtip. We were both at idle with our speed brakes out - just coasting.

He looked over at me, raised his hand and shook his fist. I thought "This is like a movie. This can't be happening!" He had on a leather flying helmet with no oxygen mask. It had evidently been sucked off when I shot his canopy away.

Then he made a 90 degree turn back to the right. Before I realized what was happening, we went between two hangers! He had led me right onto Tak Tung Kau Airfield! Red 2 was shouting again "Lead, they're shooting at us!" The flak was bursting all around us. In fact, you could see the gun barrels flashing because we were right on the deck, thirty-five miles inside China! He had gone up and down the river, leading me to the airfield figuring the flak would chase me off.

He made a turn and went down the runway. He seemed to be trying to force his aircraft down for a landing. But he hadn't lowered his gear and he was still doing about 300 knots, but so low that he was blowing dust off the runway. I wasn't down low enough to hit him, so I just stayed where I was knowing that he'd have to pull up or make a turn. When

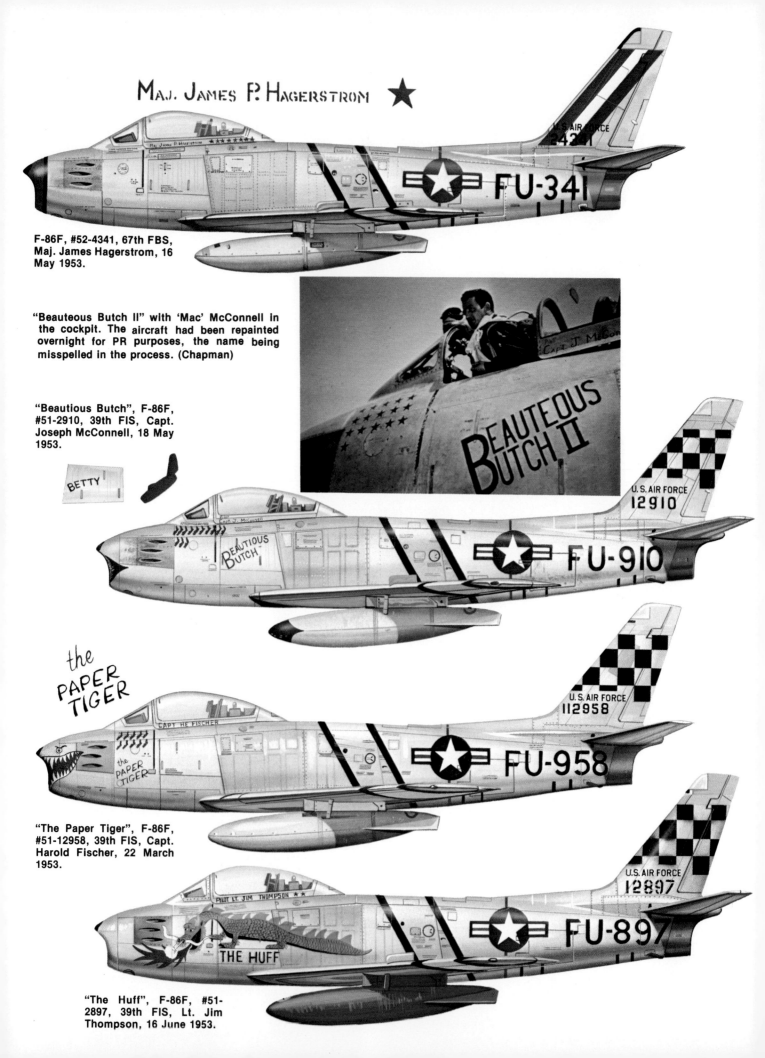

MAJ. JAMES P. HAGERSTROM ★

F-86F, #52-4341, 67th FBS, Maj. James Hagerstrom, 16 May 1953.

"Beauteous Butch II" with 'Mac' McConnell in the cockpit. The aircraft had been repainted overnight for PR purposes, the name being misspelled in the process. (Chapman)

"Beautious Butch", F-86F, #51-2910, 39th FIS, Capt. Joseph McConnell, 18 May 1953.

"The Paper Tiger", F-86F, #51-12958, 39th FIS, Capt. Harold Fischer, 22 March 1953.

"The Huff", F-86F, #51-2897, 39th FIS, Lt. Jim Thompson, 16 June 1953.

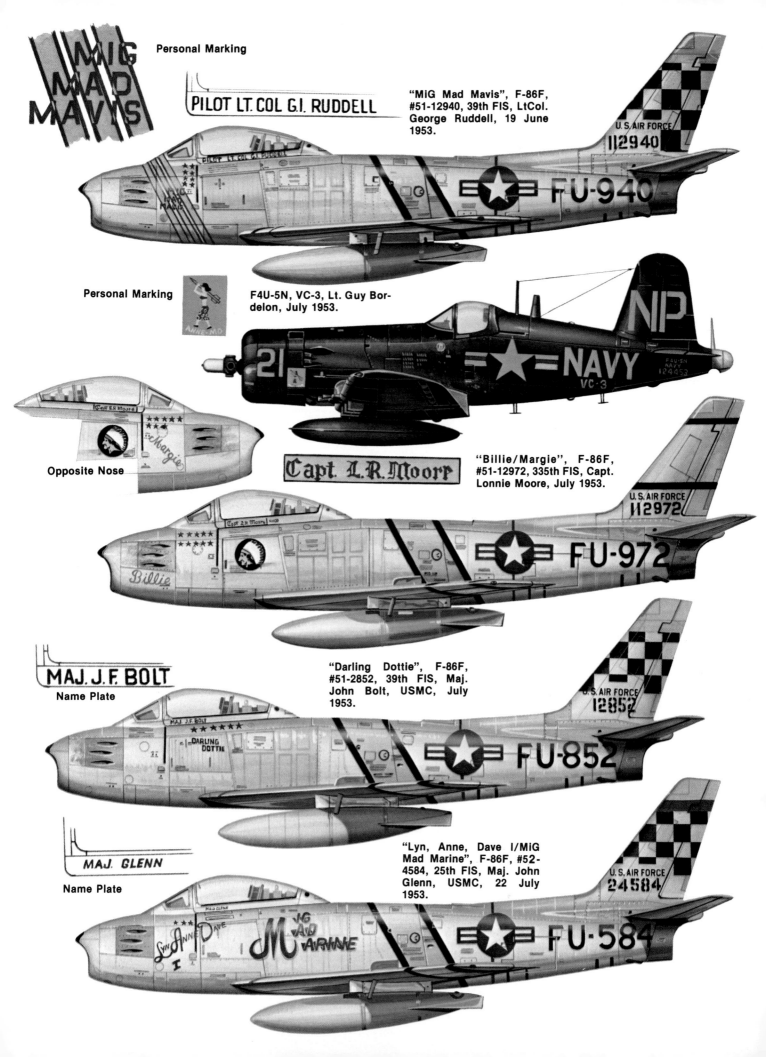

Personal Marking

PILOT LT. COL G.I. RUDDELL

"MiG Mad Mavis", F-86F, #51-12940, 39th FIS, LtCol. George Ruddell, 19 June 1953.

U.S. AIR FORCE
112940
FU-940

Personal Marking

ANNE M.O

F4U-5N, VC-3, Lt. Guy Bordelon, July 1953.

NP
21
NAVY
VC-3
F4U-5N
NAVY
124453

Opposite Nose

Capt. E.R. Moore
Margie

Capt. L.R. Moore

"Billie/Margie", F-86F, #51-12972, 335th FIS, Capt. Lonnie Moore, July 1953.

U.S. AIR FORCE
112972
Capt. L.R. Moore
Billie
FU-972

MAJ. J.F. BOLT

Name Plate

"Darling Dottie", F-86F, #51-2852, 39th FIS, Maj. John Bolt, USMC, July 1953.

MAJ. J.F. BOLT
DARLING DOTTIE
U.S. AIR FORCE
12852
FU-852

MAJ. GLENN

Name Plate

"Lyn, Anne, Dave I/MiG Mad Marine", F-86F, #52-4584, 25th FIS, Maj. John Glenn, USMC, 22 July 1953.

MAD GLENN
Lyn Anne Dave
I
MiG Mad Marine
U.S. AIR FORCE
24584
FU-584

Four Aces - James Low, Robby Risner, Royal Baker, and Leonard Lilley - of the 4th FIW in November 1952. (USAF)

he did, I really hammered him. I blew about four feet off his left wing. It exploded in fire. When that happened he made a hard right chandelle, then a right turn back down and parallel to the runway. He was probably trying to make it in the grass alongside the runway.

I fired all the rest of my ammunition into him. He leveled off, still doing about 350 knots, touched the ground and came unglued. Little pieces flew everywhere.

The *MiG* was finally down but this mission was far from being over. As we climbed away from Tak Tung Kau, we had to pass right over Antung. We had been told that they had about 250 radar-controlled anti-aircraft guns in this area and they were right. The flak was everywhere. Red 2 got hit in the belly and began to lose fuel. When he was down to 5 minutes fuel, I told him to shut down and I would try to push him.

Tucking the nose of my aircraft right up his tailpipe, I pushed him all the way to Cho-do Island in the Yellow Sea, where we had a rescue operation. He made it with room to spare, and bailed out near the island. I landed at K-14 with the nose of my bird all boogered up. That evening we went to the airplane to meet Red 2. When they opened the doors, he didn't get off. He had drowned.

In October the *MiGs* returned to the 'fly high, fast, and many' tactics they had been using back in 1951. With the new *F-86Fs* available, the 4th and 51st tacticians came up with some new wrinkles to help the *"86"* pilots. First they went to larger flight sizes to counter the larger *MiG* formations. The 51st went to 6 ship flights and the 4th used 8. Then they staggered the altitudes so as to be ready for the *MiGs* at whatever altitude they chose. With the *F-86Es* patrolling at from 30-35,000 feet, and the *Fs* at 42-45,000 feet, they ended the month with 27 *MiGs* destroyed against a loss of one *F-84* and 4 *F-86s*.

Some *F-86As* were painted OD in an effort to deceive the *MiGs*. All that was accomplished was a loss of some 20mph top speed. (AFM)

Capt. Chuck Owens claimed 9 *MiGs* in "El Diablo" (Ebersole)

The 67th TRW camouflaged some of their *RG-80s* but this too proved ineffective. (Garrett)

67th TRW *RF-80s* got *F-86* escort on all missions into *MiG* Alley. (USAF)

November and December saw the *MiGs* trying similar tactics. They would make almost no aggressive moves toward the *86s* and only attacked the fighter-bombers if it was a sure thing. Still, in November, 28 *MiGs* were destroyed and three new aces crowned - Col. Royal "King" Baker, Capt. Leonard Lilley, and Capt. Cecil Foster. On 18 November, some *Panther* pilots from the **USS Oriskany**, flying top cover for *AD* strikes on Hoeryong in extreme northeast Korea, were attacked by **Russian** *MiG 15s* from bases near Vladivostok. The *Panthers* shot down one of the *MiGs* and the rest ran for home.

The "Scoshi Chief" was the combat orientation aircraft of the 4th FIW. (Brewer)

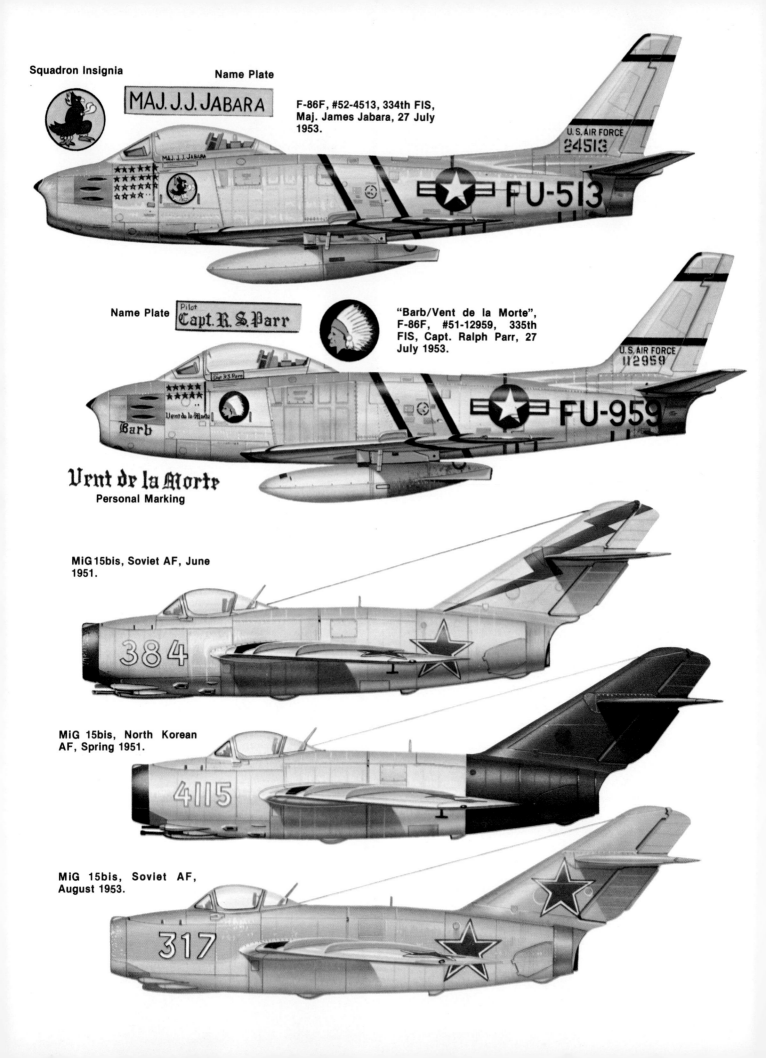

Squadron Insignia

Name Plate

MAJ. J. J. JABARA

F-86F, #52-4513, 334th FIS, Maj. James Jabara, 27 July 1953.

MAJ. J. J. JABARA

U.S. AIR FORCE
24513

FU-513

Name Plate Pilot Capt. R. S. Parr

"Barb/Vent de la Morte", F-86F, #51-12959, 335th FIS, Capt. Ralph Parr, 27 July 1953.

Capt. R. S. Parr

Vent de la Morte

Barb

U.S. AIR FORCE
112959

FU-959

Vent de la Morte

Personal Marking

MiG 15bis, Soviet AF, June 1951.

384

MiG 15bis, North Korean AF, Spring 1951.

4115

MiG 15bis, Soviet AF, August 1953.

317

Part of the 9 kills on "Elenore" belong to Maj. William Whisner of WWII fame. (USAF)

Lt. Cecil Foster
7 Sept. 1952, 16th FIS, F-86E
No. 51-2868

It was our flights' day off and I was walking through the 16th FIS Ops building, dressed in my service blues and carrying my camera, when I overheard the Ops Officer answer the field telephone from Group Ops. Group wanted another flight to sit 5 minute alert. They had just scrambled the 25th FIS alert birds and needed a stand-by flight until the 25th could recover and turn around four more aircraft.

Lt. Sands, "A" Flight Commander, was in the building briefing some new pilots when the Ops Officer ordered him to assume alert status **asap**. Lt. Sands had plenty of wingmen available but no certified Element Leader. I had been certified as an Element Leader a few days prior but hadn't flown as such yet.

The Ops Officer ordered me to get dressed and fill in until someone else was available. I started running for the locker room to change when the call came "Scramble!" Lt. Sands and the wingmen had a two minute head start on me. But while I was strapping in, some friends of mine did a fast 'pre-flight' and another straddled the nose, reached in the cockpit and started my engine. I was the third airplane to reach the 'active', gunned the engine and closed the canopy

on the takeoff roll.

Immediately after takeoff, Lt. Sands had to abort because he couldn't raise his landing gear. Because of the emergency of the situation, someone had forgotten to reset the manual gear extension system in the preflight and his gear couldn't retract. Lt. Sands and his wingman were forced to return to K-13.

I assumed command and we proceeded toward the mouth of the Yalu. As we passed Cho-Do, I called for us to orbit there until our drop tanks went dry. Listening to our tactical frequency, I could easily tell that the *MiGs* were up in force. With the sky perfectly clear, we could see the many contrails near the Yalu and many more forming. We'd been airborne about 30 minutes when the tanks went dry and we 'cleaned' up the airplanes.

We were at 40,000 feet when I spotted 8 aircraft level with us, flying in elements of two in trail. Since our side flew either flights of 4 or elements of 2, I knew it was 8 *MiGs*. I began moving to their six o'clock. We'd now been airborne about 35 minutes.

The *MiG* leader had also seen us and began a smooth level left turn. I was able to cut them off in the turn and happily approaching a stern position. Suddenly, the *MiGs* began a zoom climb to an altitude that the *F-86* could not reach.

At the same time, Lt Erickson called out *"MiGs* at 6 o'clock high!"*. It was another flight of eight. Their altitude gave them the speed advantage so I performed a maximum performance left turn. As they slid by on the outside, I barrel-rolled back to the right, putting me about at their 7 o'clock.

My attention came back to the first flight of MiGs which had continued to orbit in a left descending turn. The action seemed to be in slow motion because at 40,000 feet, the rarified atmosphere requires a feather touch on the stick to maintain airspeed and altitude. At this altitude, the entire orbit had a diameter of about 30 miles!

As I began to get into position on the first MiG flight, my wingman called a third MiG flight descending and coming to our 6 o'clock. Taking defensive action, I could observe all 24 MiGs. We had no trouble picking out the bad guys as we two were the only good guys in the area. This cat and mouse game continued for some time with both my wingman and myself getting off a burst of fire occasionally.

We felt that we had the MiGs 'cornered' because we were always near the stern position of one of the MiG flights. Two of the MiG flights could safely disengage but that would leave the third flight in an unfavorable position. Periodically checking my fuel, I soon realized that we only had a few more minutes before we'd have to break off.

Suddenly, Lt. Erickson said "Lead, did you switch sides?", meaning did I look to the opposite side that the MiGs were on. I hadn't so I snapped my head to the right and saw a lone MiG closing at our 3 o'clock. I immediately gave up my pursuit of the three flights of MiGs and performed a roll that placed me about 1200 feet behind the loner. It was a perfect set-up.

I put the pipper on his aircraft and fired a good long burst. There were sparkles as the API bullets scored hits on the wings and fuselage. Realigning my aircraft, I fired again but he was out at about 2000 feet by now. There were a few more hits but the MiG continued to fly straight ahead and descending. I had lost some speed maneuvering to get behind the MiG and lost a bit more from the recoil of the guns. When Lt. Erickson called "Bingo", I put the sight on the MiG again and started firing a burst before he got completely out of range.

"Break Left Lead!", called Erickson. "MiGs close and firing!" One of the MiG flights had pulled in behind us and was pouring it to us. We broke left and down, did a Split S and came through the bottom at maximum speed heading for home. Keeping maximum speed until assured we were clear of MiGs, we then climbed back to 45,000 and went home. Checking the clock, I was startled to see that we had been continually engaged for 43 minutes. I claimed a 'probable' on the loner, and Lt. Erickson got a damage. Three weeks later, the claims board reviewed the claim and, using further information, upgraded my claim to 'confirmed kill'.

1Lt. Cecil Foster
26 September 1952, 16th FIS, F-86E No. 51-2868
"Tiger 3"

The mission for 26 September was a top cover mission on some fighter-bombers making a strike near the mouth of the Yalu river. I was flying No.868 which had just arrived at K-13. It had undergone its acceptance check but hadn't been harmonized at the firing range yet. We needed every plane that was in commission that day, so I happened to get 868. Upon becoming airborne, I joined Tiger Lead in a line abreast position for our enroute flight checks and the arming of our 6 .50 cal. guns. We climbed to 38,000ft as we headed straight for the mouth of the Yalu. It was a very clear day with non-persistant contrails above 35,000 ft. I was positioned to the right and high on Tiger Lead. At the mouth of the river, we turned NNE flying a course parallel to the river. We knew from the radio chatter that the MiGs had decided to come up, so we 'cleaned' our external tanks when they became empty.

About 30 miles inland, 2 MiG 15s crossed our nose heading SSE and about 3 or 4,000 feet low. Tiger Lead called the bandits and began a hard descending right turn. Being high and on the right, I had to start a left rolling turn with the intent of ending in a position to cover the rear of Tiger Lead. However, about one second after starting to turn left, I spotted 6 pairs of 'cloud spots'. I immediately recognized it as fuel coming from jettisoned drop tanks. There were 6 MiGs

flying high cover for the 2 MiGs that were being used as 'live bait'. I went right through our formation and started a scissors to the right, calling for Tiger 4 to hang on and keep me in sight. The MiG leader began a hard left turn when he spotted me so that he and his wingman were in a scissors with my wingman and myself. He began firing much too soon.

I knew I had myself a handful and I called Tiger Lead that I was in a scissors with 6 MiGs and could use a 'little help'. I saw that I had the inside radius advantage and rolled my wings level momentarily, guessed about the 'Kentucky Windage' required, and fired about a one second burst. I saw my tracers proceeding out from my nose as if they were in slow motion. They appeared to pass just behind the MiG leader's aircraft and right into the fuselage of his wingman. I saw smoke start from the MiG's tail and called "I've hit one of them" and simultaneously observed a tremendous explosion where the MiG leader was. I pulled back real hard on the stick to get into position on the wounded MiG and did a wingover at the top while calling Tiger Lead that I saw the MiG leader explode. He replied "Roger, I saw the explosion!"

I was then in a near vertical dive at the damaged MiG, and began firing at him at about 1500 ft range. Then I realized that he was floating like a maple leaf, completely out of control and inverted. I had to turn my wings so that my right wing passed between the MiG's wing and his fuselage. This scared the hell out of me as I almost rammed him. As soon as I cleared the MiG, I pulled back hard on the stick and recovered from the dive. I saw a parachute! The pilot of the second MiG had ejected. Calling "Tiger 4, are you still with me?", he replied "You're clear Tiger 3!" I then flew toward the pilot in the chute to make certain that my wingman could verify that the second MiG was shot down. I saw a long red streamer hanging vertically from the pilot in the chute. I believe that the pilot had forgotten to disconnect his low altitude ejection lanyard and when he ejected at about 38,000 ft, his chute opened automatically. He had no mask on and without oxygen and that slow descent through the extremely cold atmosphere, I assume that he most probably died.

The fireball from the MiG leader could be seen for literally hundreds of miles as the sky was completely clear until he exploded and that formed a cloud that remained for quite some time. After landing, I asked my wingman, 2ndLt. Al Grenz, who only had one mission under his belt, how he managed to stay with me. He replied "You weren't about to leave me up there alone with all those MiGs! I fixed my eyes to your tail and never looked away. You weren't about to lose me!!" After the flight, F-86E No.868 went to the firing range for gun harmonization where it was discovered that one gun was firing well to the left and it was one that had no tracers. It had actually riddled the MiG leader until he exploded. Two MiGs with one burst! What a stroke of luck!

December saw the MiG pilots starting to work together as a team. They evidently felt that since it worked for the 86 pilots, it might work for them also. MiG wingmen started covering their leader's tails much tighter. So much tighter that the F-86 pilots had trouble staying with a MiG long enough to get a 'confirmed' kill. Then the MiGs started working on a 'box-in' tactic by sending some MiGs across the river to lie in wait for the Sabres, to start home. As soon as "Bingo Fuel" was called by the Sabres, and the 86s would start to withdraw, MiGs that had been waiting across the Yalu would jump them. The MiGs lying in wait would immediately go to a line abreast formation and 'box-in' the retiring Sabres. Without the UN GCI radars warning the Sabres of the MiG ambushes, it could have been costly. As it was, more than a few Sabres were lost, not to MiGs, but to fuel starvation, forcing a bailout over friendly territory. Only 2 Sabres were shot down, costing the Reds 28 MiGs.

In January 1953 another class of MiG drivers 'graduated' from the Antung Air Academy. Some 2200 MiG sorties were counted, with 650 of them actually doing battle with the Sabres. But these were not ordinary MiG pilots. Even their aircraft were different from the others. Painted a coppery tan on the upper surfaces and sky blue on the under, these guys were tough. When a 'train' of MiGs would cross the Yalu, these pilots initiated combat with the Sabres. They demonstrated good flight integrity, used good tactics, and had a superior aircraft. Still they only got two confirmed kills while losing 39 of their own. Two more names were added to the Ace List - Capt. Dolph Overton and Capt. Harold Fischer.

"This'll Kill Ya" is the "Lady Margaret" renamed. The "Lady" held the World Speed Record. (Chapman)

Capt. Cecil Foster standing by his aircraft "Three Kings". The aircraft was later named "Four Kings & A Queen" after Capt. Foster's fourth son was born. Capt. Foster shot down nine MiGs. (Foster)

Capt. Harold Fischer
15 February 1953, 39th FIS, F-86F No. 51-12958
"Charlie Lead"

We were flying a close escort mission over a strike force of F-84s that were slated to knock out the Suiho dam complex once again. Since the strike was so close to the airfields at Antung, Hqtrs had put up a force of over 80 F-86s to counter the MiG threat. The MiGs came up and it wasn't long before a big fight had developed and I soon found myself flying line-abreast with a MiG a few hundred feet away.

Immediately both of us started to scissor, each trying to get on the other's tail by turning into and then away from each other. The flight paths of both our aircraft resembled an interlacing pattern. For a few moments the situation was static with neither side having the advantage, then I took a calculated risk. One of the things a pilot should not do, theoretically, was to drop his speed brakes for this would reduce his speed, which could always be converted into altitude and the one that had the altitude had the advantage. But this situation could go on longer than I liked since there were so many other aircraft in the area. Dropping the speed brakes for a short time, my airplane fell in behind the MiG. Seeing that the advantage was on my side, the MiG headed for the border, just a few miles away. His aircraft was causing heavy contrails to form immediately and I was 600 feet behind. The contrails were so heavy that when I pulled up to shoot, my canopy would enter his contrails. The radar gunsight was working marvelously and the first burst of a few

"Laura-Ann", one of the new *F-86F-30s* with which the 18th FBW was re-equipped. *F-30s* could carry the standard load of 2 drop tanks and six .50s plus two 1,000lb bombs. (Menard)

Major James Hagerstrom, CO of the 67th FBS, was the only fighter-bomber pilot to make 'ace', getting two *MiGs* in the 4th FIW and 6 more in the 18th FBW. (USAF)

seconds caused his aircraft to light up almost from wingtip to wingtip. It seemed that every round found its mark. Before I had a chance to fire again, the canopy came off and the pilot came out.

As soon as I saw the pilot was bailing out I called my wingman and asked him if he saw it. Replying in the affirmative, I looked over to see his position. He was off to my left and slightly higher. Looking at him and the *MiGs* in front of us, I saw him fire and the right wingroot of the *MiG* sparkled with an excellent hit. It was his first mission deep into enemy territory and it was already a success. Before he had a chance to press his advantage he called for me to break since I had a *MiG* on my tail ready to fire. Looking over my shoulder, a shiver of fear coursed through my frame. There about 1500 feet out at about seven o'clock was a single *MiG*. Rolling up and over, I pulled as many Gs inverted as I could without stalling the aircraft and losing my airspeed. Then doing a Split S, I called my wingman again asking if he was still there. He replied that he wasn't and that he had lost me and was heading for home. Checking my tail, I too started for home.

Looking above, I saw a lone *F-86* heading to the south, which I assumed was my lost wingman. Behind him was another airplane, a *MiG*, and he was about 3000 feet dead

astern of the *F-86*. Now it became the hunted stalking the hunter. I took up position about 3000 feet directly behind the *MiG*. Calling the *F-86* pilot, I told him of the *MiG* and called for him to level off, build up speed and run for it. He acknowledged and I saw both him and the *MiG* ease down. I called him again and told him I would call the breaks as I initiated my attack. I also assured him that he was in little danger from the *MiG* due to the range. Knowing that the *MiG* would have to turn sometime to go back to his base, I was in an excellent position for an attack even if I was out of range at the time.

Nearing the Chongchon River, my range on the *MiG* had decreased. Checking my own six o'clock, I saw that I was also being followed at a long distance. It was easy to determine *MiGs* from *Sabres* since our airplanes were now in the heavy contrail area. Squeezing off a few bursts, the *MiG* in front of me finally became aware of my presence, or possibly one of the other *MiGs* warned him by radio. He began a turn to the left and I fell in behind in a turn to decrease the distance between our two aircraft. The *MiG* pilot tried their successful tactic of zooming but in a turn this was not as successful as usual and I ended up 30 feet behind him almost in a full stall. The *MiG* in front of me was a beautiful silver color, looking almost factory fresh. At this range, I couldn't miss and squeezed the trigger. The burst hit directly behind the cockpit and caused it to light up in an encircling glare of light. He immediately snapped into a spin and there was nothing for me to do but spin with him. Both of us went into the spin at 38,000 feet and, squeezing off a burst in the spin, I was able to register another hit on his wingtip. His was a spin that continued all the way to the ground.

As soon as the second hit registered, I pulled out of the spin and looked around. From my left came the *MiG* that had been following me and attempting to do the same thing to me that I had done to his compatriot. In this case, his position was not as good as mine had been. Turning into him, he slid on by and I again turned so that I was behind him. His speed was too great and he pulled away rapidly. When our speeds stabilized, he was out of range at about 4,000 feet. Other kills had been made at this range so I concentrated on firing at the fleeing *MiG*. My wingman was now calling "Bingo" but I told him to hold on a moment more and I squeezed off a burst. Calling my wingman to start for home, I fired all my ammunion at the *MiG* and finally left him as he crossed over into Manchuria.

February saw the aggressive *MiGs* still in the air but now making a lot of mistakes. They started penetrating too far south and at too low an altitude and ended up 'meat on the table'. Only above 40,000 feet did a *MiG* have any advantages over the *Sabre* and these guys were down around 25,000 feet where the *Sabre* worked best.

Project GUNVAL sent ten F-86F-2s to Korea re-armed with four 20mm cannon. Although they had many problems, they did get credit for 6 confirmed kills. (Miller)

The month of February also saw the beginning of the race for the title of top scoring ace in Korea. The late Major George Davis was then leader with 14 *MiGs*, followed by Col. Royal Baker with 13. Capt. Joseph McConnell got his 5th *MiG* on 16 February. James Jabara, now a Major, had returned for another tour and brought with him a record of 6 *MiGs*. In a fight over Suiho Reservoir on 18 February, four *F-86s* 'jumped' 48 *MiGs*. When the fight was over 2 *MiGs* had been shot down and two others had crashed trying to evade the 'crazy Americans'. The two *MiGs* shot down were credited to Capt. Manuel 'Pete' Fernandez. These last three pilots would race for the title.

Capt. Manuel 'Pete' Fernandez
10 May 1953, F-86F, No. 51-2857, 334th FIS
"John Dog 1"

On May 9th, we were told in the evening that we would be on a day fighter sweep to the Yalu. I was overjoyed as I hadn't drawn a fighter sweep for a couple of weeks. But in the morning, they told us that we were to intercept and escort a large flight of *F-84s*. They would be going to the Yalu to bomb an electrical generating plant and we would provide the top cover. Naturally I was upset to lose out on the fighter sweep but as it worked out it was a very busy day.

I was leading the flight, Lt. Richard Maroney on my wing. The mission airborne commander was Major Foster Smith, who would eventually end up with 4½ *MiGs*. We took off at lengthy intervals due to adverse weather conditions and proceeded north to the rendezvous point. There was solid cloud cover all the way from K-14 to the rendezvous. Plans were for us to drop out of the clouds near the ChongChon River where the *F-84s* would be waiting.

When we broke out, the *84s* were just in front of us and I started an extremely high speed sweep over the top and from side to side over the *84s*. This was just my flight as the rest of the flights were nowhere in sight. I contacted the *F-84* leader and told him that we would cover him and we proceeded to the target area.

Just as we arrived over the target, about 48 *MiGs* hit us with some of them trying to break through and get at the *84s*. I pulled in behind one of them trying to break through. He and his wingman pulled up and to the left in a futile attempt to evade us. I put the pipper on the lead *MiG's* fuselage and gave him a good heavy burst. He immediately caught fire and exploded.

Breaking away I lined up on the *MiG* wingman and put a good burst into his tail. He also started streaming smoke and fire. I then heard Moroney call "Dog Lead, I've got a *MiG* on my tail! And he's firing!" I broke off from behind the No. 2

53

Red Airfields

Manchuria

"MiG Alley"

(Map labels: Mukden, Hoeryong, Chongjin, Hyesanjin, Hoemun, Kilchu, Kanggye, Kuantien, Fengcheng, Antung, Tafung, Kou, Uiju, Sinuiju, Koto-Ri, Namsi, Teachon, Saamcham, Anju, Sinanju, Hamhung, Tonpo, Sondok, Takushan, Wonsan, P. East, P. Downtown, P. Main, Pyongyang, Anak, Sariwon, Pyonggang, Sinmak, Haeju, Suwon, Kimpo, 38th Parallel, Yalu River, Chongchon River)

"Barbara", presumed to be one of Capt. Ralph Parr's aircraft. Note unusual drop tank paint treatment, red in color. (Taylor via Menard)

Capt. Ralph Parr shows the new Vice President where the tape deck is in an *F-86*. (USAF)

MiG (an unofficial kill) and went to help Moroney.

I started to call the breaks "Dog 2, Break right!" Moroney broke right and the *MiG* followed. Then I saw another *F-86* far behind the fight and completely out of range, but firing furiously. When Moroney and the *MiG* broke right, I pulled up high to lose forward speed and came down behind the *MiG*. The other *F-86* was behind me but not close enough in range where I would be threatened by his guns.

I gave the *MiG* a good short burst which killed his engine. But again I had to break off because Moroney had another *MiG* chasing him. Moroney was right beside the *MiG* when I hit him and saw everything. About this time I noticed that we were on Bingo fuel so decided that we should head for home. Besides, Moroney was working me to death!

When we got home, Major Smith said it was he that was in the other *F-86* firing over my head at the *MiG* and that he was claiming half of the 'kill'. I put in for a probable, which was later upgraded to a confirmed and Major Smith and I shared the 'kill'. That made 14½ *MiGs* for me.

In March, the Reds made an attempt to put *MiG* air cover over the front lines, which were at the 38th Parallel. Using underwing tanks, the *MiGs* came down and engaged the *Sabres* over Sariwon, Chinampo, and Sinmak. The Sinmak battle was only 38 miles from the front. But again, they had to come down to where the *F-86s* performed at their best, around 20,000 feet, and the *Sabres* had a field day. 34 *MiGs* were shot down while only 2 *Sabres* were lost.

The 18th Fighter Bomber Wing had converted to the *F-86F* in February. But until they had enough proficiency in flying and bombing in the *F-86*, they would fly combat patrols in *MiG* Alley. With the 67th being commanded by Major James Hagerstrom, this was an easy task. Major Hagerstrom had two *MiGs* to his credit from his time in the 4th FIW. On *MiGCAP* Patrols in late February and early March he would become an Ace, getting his 5th *MiG* on 27 March. He was the only ace from a non-intercepter unit. Col. James K. Johnson and LtCol. George 'Red' Jones also got No. 5 in March to become Aces No. 29 and 30 in Korea. And 'Pete' Fernandez got 4 more *MiGs* to become a 'double'.

Spring of 1953 brought two items to the *F-86* pilots that sealed the fate of the *MiGs*. For some time it had been recognized that the one thing the *Sabres* lacked was the hitting power of the *MiG* cannon. You could literally sieve a *MiG* with the *Sabre* .50 calibres and it might not go down. But one hit from a *MiG's* 23mm cannon shell could take out a *Sabre*. Under Project GUNVAL, 10 *F-86Es* and *Fs* were modified to carry four 20mm cannon in place of the six .50 calibres. The guns worked quite well but the actual conversion didn't. Originally, gun gas was purged by a small door that opened into the intake area. Unfortunately when the exhaust doors were opened for an extended burst of fire, compressor stall or 'flameout' would often occur. The very first GUNVAL mission saw the loss of the *Sabre* due to compressor stall. And the *MiG* got away! A quick field mod welded the intake doors shut and gas buildup was relieved by drilling 4 holes in the gunbay doors. The next problem was the lack of an adequate ammo storage area. The reworked .50 calibre bays could only hold enough ammo for a 4 second burst from each gun. Finally, a switch was installed allowing the pilot to fire only two guns at one time, thus giving him eight seconds total firing time. The tests of the guns were deemed successful with six *MiGs* destroyed and three probables. The GUNVAL airplanes were only flown by veteran pilots and some of the kills were by Major Vermont Garrison, Capt. Lonnie Moore, and LtCol. George Jones. The guns were standardized as the M-39 'high speed 20mm cannon' and installed in the *F-86H*, *F-100*, and *F-101A*.

LtCol. William Cosby in the cockpit of "Funfrus". Cosby had three *MiGs* when he was CO of the 334th FIS. (USAF)

A 91st SRS *RB-45C* that was forced down at K-14 in 1953. The *RB-45s* still weren't fast enough to elude the *MiGs*. (Miller)

Anxious crewmen watch the north for the return of their pilots. "Patricia II" is 'Joltin' Joe Romack's aircraft in which he shot down two *MiGs*. (Miller)

F-86 Squadron Markings

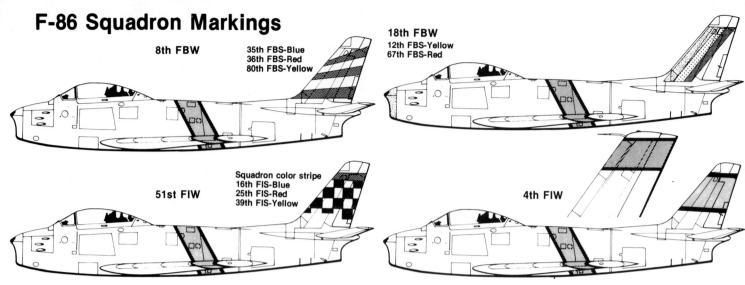

8th FBW

35th FBS-Blue
36th FBS-Red
80th FBS-Yellow

18th FBW

12th FBS-Yellow
67th FBS-Red

51st FIW

Squadron color stripe
16th FIS-Blue
25th FIS-Red
39th FIS-Yellow

4th FIW

Lt. Jim Thompson's "The Huff", one of the wilder paint schemes seen on an *F-86*. Thompson had two *MiGs*. (N-AA)

"Miss Tena" was the personal mount of Col. Wilmet while he was CO of the 8th FBW at K-13. (Wood via Garrett)

56

A 3rd Air Rescue Sq. *H-19* pulls Capt. Joe McConnell from the Yellow Sea after a *MiG* fatally damaged his first "Beautious Butch" on 12 April 1953. 'Mac' vowed to avenge the loss with at least 15 *MiGs*. (USAF)

LtCol. George L. Jones
F-86F, 335 FIS, 'GUNVAL'

In the Winter of 1952-53, several *F-86s* were fitted with 20mm cannon in an attempt to increase the effectiveness of the *F-86* in combat. The six .50 calibre machine guns of the *F-86 Sabre* did not have the hitting power needed for a quick kill. The mission for the day was to find and engage the *MiGs* and combat test the effectiveness of the new guns.

Originally, a flight of four aircraft was to take part in the mission. But somewhere along the line two didn't get off and my wingman and I proceeded on the mission. We were a flight of two, I with the 20mm armed *F-86* and lead aircraft, my wingman in a normally armed *F-86* flying cover for me. Climbing out, we crossed the no-bomb line and fired a short test burst to check the guns. They worked perfectly and we continued to the north, climbing to a patrol altitude of 35,000 feet. We maintained strict radio silence and shortly after leveling off at 35,000 we heard the rest of the mission aircraft begin checking in on the radio as they climbed out to the north on the same heading.

Flicking my left wing down for the crossover signal, I moved my wingman to the left side and gave him the 'heads up' sign. I knew there were plenty of *MiGs* somewhere in the area and I wanted no surprises. The mission plan was to use the large formation of *F-86s* behind us as a focal point of attention on the enemy radarscopes. Our small flight would therefore have a good chance to make a surprise 'bounce' on the *MiGs*.

As we approached the Yalu, I spotted a glint in the sky, about 3 o'clock high. I wagged the stick, rocking my wings to get my wingman's attention. He looked across and I silently signaled "Drop tanks!" Again a silent signal for full military power, and we started a slow turn under that 'glint' in the sky.

"Father Dan", a flight commander's aircraft in the 25th FIS. This *F-86E* originally belonged to Capt. Cecil Foster. Shark's teeth on nose were for Tiger Flight of the 25th FIS. Note the command stripe around the nose. (Taylor via Menard)

Now there were MANY other flashes in the sun up ahead.

All of a sudden I saw them. First there was nothing, then they jumped into focus. A flight of *MiGs* in loose trail, climbing as they crossed the river. Ever so gently we increased our rate of turn and started an easy climb, swinging in behind them. We were too far out to shoot. We had to close. I watched the range dial on the gunsight unroll — 2800 feet, 2600 feet, 2400 feet. We were closing but slowly. I edged around in my seat and glanced behind. Bad news! A *MiG* was almost in position to swing in for an attack on me! I now realized that I had cut between the last two aircraft in the *MiG* formation. Where was my wingman? There he was, on my right wingtip and dropping his wing as if to start a pass on the *MiG* closing on my rear. Good Boy! I snapped my head around to the left. The *MiG*, which had tilted his wing down on the start of a firing pass, suddenly straightened up and leveled out. Now I got the picture - if the *MiG* pilot jumped me, my wingman would swing in behind him. The *MiG* driver backed off.

By now, we were climbing through 40,000 feet and I was closing on the *MiG* leader. The range gate marker stood at 1800 feet. I wanted 800 feet but I wasn't sure how long the game between the two wingmen, the *MiG* leader's and mine, would keep up. Each was feinting an attack, one on me, one at the other. The range dial kept unwinding — 1600 feet, 1400 feet. In the back of my mind I kept recalling the one problem that we hadn't been able to lick with these new guns - compressor stall. At high altitude, firing the guns had resulted in several compressor stalls or 'flame-outs'. This left you a sitting duck unless you could recover by diving to a lower altitude. "The hell with it! Shoot first, worry about the stall if it comes" I thought.

The range dial now indicated 1000 feet and the *MiG* pilot on my tail was now getting frantic. For the first time during the flight, my wingman broke radio silence. "I can't hold him much longer Lead! Get out of there!" "Watch him", I said,

"Call if he begins a pass." I eased the nose of the *86* up. The sight was just under the *MiG* leader's tail. "Up a little", I thought, "Don't lose airspeed."

The sight pipper was right on his tailpipe now. The range dial at 800 feet. The little orange colored diamonds of the sight reflected on my windscreen circled the *MiG* perfectly. I pressed the trigger. Instantly a stream of bright flashes exploded in rapid succession on the *MiG* ahead. Bursting out in fire and smoke, it seemed to stop in mid-air. I was momentarily fascinated by the sight. Then with an awful start, I realized that I was about to run into him. Before I could do anything I was enveloped in the smoke. I felt there was a solid wall of debris ahead in the darkness. Instinctively I retarded the throttle, my thumb jerking back the speed brake switch. I pulled back on the stick and rolled upside down, hoping to get out of the way. Suddenly I was out of the smoke and I saw the *MiG* - canopy gone, cockpit empty. it was going down trailing smoke and fire and debris.

As I rolled upright I noticed the unmistakable sound of an engine in a compressor stall. My engine! Roaring and buzzing and vibrating the entire airframe. At this point I wasn't too worried. I knew what to do - point the nose down and get up some airspeed. In the past we had usually recovered from these stalls around 30,000 feet. But when I passed through 30,000 with the engine still stalling, I began to get nervous. 27,000 feet! 25,000 feet! And still stalling. I started thinking about emergency procedures and realized that I would have to pull out at 18,000 feet, put her into a glide and try to make the sea. But the sea looked far away!

It was then that I noticed that my speed brake switch had broken off — my speed brakes were still open and slowing me down. I pushed my index finger between the thumb guard to the nub of the switch and edged it forward. It clicked, the brakes closed, and I felt the aircraft leap forward. With the increased speed, the buzzing sound stopped, the engine smoothed - and the compressor stall broke. I eased the power on - it was 18,000 feet - and took a deep breath. I felt better now and looked around for my wingman. There he was, just off my right wingtip, staring through the oil smeared canopy at me. I started to relax a little and called him. "Let's get the hell out of here. I'll buy the drinks." "You're all heart, Lead!"

"Dragon Lady" flew many missions with the 12th TRS as the 'Hunter' in B-26 'Hunter-Killer Team' operations. (USAF)

Maj. Howard Ebersole got a *MiG* in 387, something most fighter-bomber pilots never did. Note old-style 18th FBW markings. (Ebersole)

"Bob's Buggy" from the 80th FBS. Name is in yellow edged in black, tail stripes are yellow. (Menard/Garrett)

The 18th FBW prepares to launch the May Day attack on PyongYang Radio Station, 1 May 1953. The entire *Sabre* force was involved in this raid. (NAA)

The second 'gift' to the *Sabre* drivers was the '6-3 wing'. The '6-3 wing' was a conversion that replaced the leading edge slat with a smooth, unbroken leading edge that was extended 6 inches at the wingroot and 3 inches at the wingtip. To smooth the airflow over the wing, a 6 inch high fence was added at 70% of the span. This allowed the *Sabre* to turn with the *MiG* at high altitudes, thus eliminating one of the last advantages the *MiG* had. It also increased speed and range marginally. Col. James K. Johnson, CO of the 4th Wing, reported that "performance of the *MiG* and *Sabre* were almost equal as long as the *Sabres* were well maintained." This would be proven in the last four months of the war.

April was the beginning of the end for the Reds. The weather was fine for flying which meant the *Sabres* were up in full force. Full force included a fourth F-86 wing as the 8th FBW traded their aging F-80Cs for brand new F-86F-30s. These were the fighter-bomber *Sabres* that had

weapons pylons inboard of the wing tanks. Each pylon could hold a 1,000 lb bomb. There now were two air superiority F-86 units, the 4th and 51st FIW, and two fighter-bomber F-86 units, the 8th and 18th FBW, all flying the new F-86Fs.

But again, for the most part, the *MiGs* didn't want to fight. The ones that did were plenty good as they shot down two big hunters from the 51st Wing. Capt. Harold Fischer was shot down after chasing a *MiG* north of the Yalu. Captured and imprisoned, he was not released until 1955 - two years after the end of the war. The other ace shot down was Capt. Joseph McConnell. He was hit and forced to bail out over the Yellow Sea on 12 April. An Air-Sea Rescue chopper picked him out almost immediately and 'Mac' promised to pay for his F-86 by shooting down 15 *MiG 15s*. On the 24th of April, he got number 10.

Russia starts May off with a holiday and a display of their latest military equipment. May Day 1953 saw a tremendous show of airpower for the Reds, but it was put on by the Fifth Air Force. For a week prior to May Day, General Glenn Barcus let it be known that he was challenging the Red Air Force to a fight. B-29s showered North Korea with leaflets asking, "Where is the Red Air Force?"

In an effort to reduce losses to the *MiGs*, the 67th TRW re-equipped with new *RF-86Fs*. (USAF)

Radio PyongYang had been verbally attacking 5th AF pilots by broadcasting stories of attacks being made on civilians, how the 'gangsters of 5th AF' had attacked hospitals and innocent women and children. General Barcus answered them by ordering an attack on PyongYang Radio Station for May Day, and then warning them 7 days in advance that it was coming.

On May Day morning, the entire *Sabre* force went to PyongYang. With 4th and 51st Wing *Sabres* flying top cover, the 8th and 18th FBW swept in and attacked the radio station and its power source. It looked like a practice gunnery run at Yuma AFB. The fighter-bomber *Sabres* just orbited over the city and, one by one, peeled off and dropped their bombs. General Barcus personally directed the attack from his own *F-86* "Barcus Carcus".

With the station in ruins, and Capt. McConnell, Col. Ruddell, and another 51st Wing 'hot dog' on his wing, General Barcus broadcast the following message to the North Koreans:

Attention all Communists in the PyongYang area. This is General Barcus speaking. I have a message for you from the Fifth Air Force. These attacks today against military targets in PyongYang are our response to your insulting lies over the PyongYang Radio. In the future, anytime you make derogatory remarks about the Fifth Air Force you can expect our answer with bombs against military targets in your area. The attacks will be with ever increasing severity. This is all now, but we shall be back everytime you broadcast filthy lies about the Fifth Air Force. Goodbye now. This is LtGeneral Glenn O. Barcus."

The 'ace race' really heated up in May. With the *Sabre* drivers now entering combat at 98% power, the *MiGs* could no longer run away and hide. The *F-86s* were closing on the *MiGs* before their pilots could react. Pete Fernandez got another 1½ to bring his total to 14½ and the lead. But 'Mac' McConnell got one *MiG* on the 13th, another on the 14th, and again on the 16th of May to bring his total to 'lucky 13'. Two days later, on 18 May, 'Mac' got three more to finish with 16 *MiGs*. Both he and Fernandez were grounded and rotated home on 19 May.

"Honest John", the personal aircraft of Col. Walker Mahurin. Note the multiple names - each pilot just added his marking without removing the old one. (Shaw via Buchanan)

Lt. John Ludwig flew "Miss Joan" while he was with the 335th FIS, claiming 4 *MiGs*. He is now with the F-16 program at Wright-Patterson AFB, Ohio. (Ludwig via Menard)

Capt. Joseph McConnell
18 May 1953, 39th FIS, F-86F No. 51-2910

We were slated for the morning mission and intelligence had indicated that the *MiGs* would be up in force today. At 0915K, we took off from K-13 and proceeded north to the mouth of the Yalu. Climbing to our patrol altitude of 46,000 feet, we tested our guns as soon as we crossed into enemy territory. As soon as we arrived at the mouth of the river, 'KODAK', the GCI radar on Chodo Island, called out many bandits in our sector. We started seeing them now - 10, 15, 20, at least 30.

Their GCI controller must have been asleep as a flight of 4 *MiGs* flew directly in front of us without even a hint of an aggressive move. I don't think they knew we were there. I turned left into them, then reversed my turn on the first *MiG* element. I then broke right into the second *MiG* element, again reversed my turn and lined up on the No. 2 *MiG* of the first element. Lining him up in the pipper, I started to pour fire into his fuselage. The *MiG* rolled over and dived for the ground. I followed, firing occasionally until I saw the canopy come off and the pilot bail out. I watched the *MiG* crash far below.

In the process of chasing the No. 2 *MiG,* his leader had gotten on my tail. Man, he was close! I could hear the cannon just thumping away at me. The tracers from a *MiG's* cannon look like great big balls of fire heading your way - GREAT BIG! They were bouncing all around me after the *MiG* leader got on my tail for a flash. I was really kicking that *Sabre* around just trying to keep those balls of fire away. It was then that I pulled into a very high 'G' turn, reversed rolling over the top, and ended the roll at the *MiG* leader's 6 o'clock. The *MiG* continued to turn and I again had to pull very high 'Gs' to get into position to fire. I started pulling lead on the *MiG* and opened fire, hitting him in the engine and tail section. Suddenly, there was an explosion in the *MiG* engine and pieces started coming off the tail. The *MiG* rolled out and I started firing from passes descending and ascending up and down through his smoke and jet wash.

At one time while coming up through the *MiG* jet wash and smoke, still firing, the *MiG* pulled up. When I was coming out of the smoke, I saw that I was about to collide with him. I pulled up over the tail and half rolled to keep the *MiG* in sight. The pilot looked up at me and pulled up into me as though to ram me. I pushed forward violently to avoid hitting him and finally rolled out at 6 o'clock again. The *MiG* then snapped over and spun in.

About this time, all hell broke loose. *MiGs* were coming at us from all over the sky and we were all on 'Bingo fuel'. We turned and headed south, diving to pick up more speed and beat a hasty retreat back to our 'sanctuary' at K-13. But the

LtCol. George Ruddell marks his 5th kill in the gundust on the nose of "*MiG* Mad Mavis", 18 May 1953. (Chapman)

day was not over for us.

We were slated to fly the afternoon mission also. So at 1400K, our squadron took off for another foray into *MiG* Alley. It was to be exactly like the morning mission - climb to 45,000 feet, patrol the Yalu River border and wait for the *MiGs* to come up. They did but they brought some of their 'Honchos' along this afternoon. You could tell by the way they worked some of their formations.

They tried to decoy me in a neat trick, but their timing was off. It's called the 'hit and run'. A flight of four *MiGs* would break down into the two elements with the first element diving down on us and intentionally overshooting. While we were attempting to pull into a firing position on the first element, the second would come down and close rapidly on us from 6 o'clock. This time I was sure it was a set-up and I followed. They lost their timing and I jumped on the tail of one of them and really poured the fire to him. Smoke came from his tail and I ploughed right through it. The *MiG* then pulled up, opened his speed brakes and bailed out. It must be a trend now. Maybe they're giving medals for it — five bail-outs and you get to be an ace. Another *MiG* then came at me and I had to break for the rest of my flight.

LtGen. Glenn O. Barcus, CO of FEAF Fighter Command, and the "Barcus Carcus" in which he flew 13 combat missions. Stars denote his rank, not *MiG* kills. (Chapman)

Two 319th FIS *F-94Bs* on patrol over North Korea. By war's end, 319th pilots had claimed 4 *MiGs*. (Chapman)

One that didn't get away. Note Yalu River under *MiG* nose. (USAF)

LtCol. George Ruddell, CO of the 39th 'Cobra' Squadron, got another *MiG* on 18 May to become ace No. 31. Major James Jabara got in a few licks when he led a flight of *Sabres* right through 16 *MiGs*. He forced one into a fatal spin, shot down another for his 8th and 9th kills. *MiGs* fell at the rate of 56 to 1 in May. FEAF announced a new tactic - "A new, inexpensive, highly efficient 'MiG Killer' technique has been found! If the *MiG* pilot sees you, he bails out; if he doesn't see you, you shoot him down! What could be more effective?"

June was even worse for the *MiG* pilots. It was obvious by their inflight actions that the pilots seen in June were not the 'Honchos'. They made pitiful mistakes. Two of them rammed each other trying to evade a chasing *Sabre*. *MiGs* simply lost control and spun in. Sometimes the pilot would just try to hide behind his armor plate and take no evasive action at all. This resulted in the *F-86* simply shooting the *MiG* to pieces. The Russian instructors must have left at 'mid-term'!

Five aces were crowned in June, most of any month of the war. Col. Vermont Garrison, Capt. Lonnie Moore, and Capt. Ralph Parr, all from the 335th FIS, and Col. Robert Baldwin and Lt. Henry Buttlemann from the 51st Wing all made ace. And Major Jabara jumped right back into the 'ace race' with five *MiGs* to bring his total to 14. The record for the month of June 1953 was ridiculous — 77 *MiGs* destroyed with no *Sabres* lost in air-to-air combat.

Capt. Ralph Parr
F-86F No. 51-12959, 335th FIS, "John Shark 4"

Early on 7 June 1953, I went down to the 335th FIS Operations Room with the other 'new sports'. It was just 8am and I found my name on the morning fighter sweep. I was flying number 4 slot in John Shark Flight. Flight commander was 1Lt. Mervin Ricker, LtCol. Robert Dixon no. 2, 2Lt. Al Cox leading the element and myself as no. 4. The flight sat together in the briefing room at Group Ops and got the full briefing on the mission. As the group briefing broke up, we then went back to 335th Ops and had a lengthy flight briefing

to cover how we would operate, procedures, possible emergencies, etc. One of the instructions for the day was to head for home if we couldn't maintain a flight of four, as lately the *MiGs* had been flying in larger formations.

On the way out to the aircraft, Al Cox told me that in as much as I had a heavy fighter background, 165 missions in *F-80s*, if I called a bounce or enemy contact that he couldn't pick up immediately, he would clear me to lead and he would take the number four slot. We climbed straight out in a spread formation, nearly line abreast. Crossing the invisible bomb line, we armed our guns and checked our sights. The weather was clear and beautiful and we reached our assigned altitude of 43,000 ft. just as our drop tanks went dry. We set up our flight pattern parallel to the Yalu and about 20 miles south of the river. "Romeo", our GCI center at Seoul, called out that they had bandit tracks in our area. John Shark Lead immediately called "Drop tanks!".

On our second wing to the northeast, I was on the extreme right side. Looking into the flight, I saw a flight of *MiGs* coming down on us at an incredible closure rate from the left. I called "John Shark, break left! *MiGs* close and firing!" I kept my eyes glued to Cox during the break to keep from losing him, and after making a 180° turn, he rolled out and I skidded it out line abreast, all the time trying to look eight places at once! The *MiGs* had come in at 90° and played hit and run with no damage to any of us. John Shark Lead had gone to the right after the *MiGs* but they kept on going 'til out of sight.

Since we had separated into two flights of two during the break, Lead told Shark 3 to start his withdrawal from the area. Cox decided we would finish our present course before swinging for home. We had lost about three thousand feet during the break and were now nursing our way back to 41,000ft, when I looked to my right, down on the river, and saw some movement. I called it out as being very low and Al Cox came right back saying "I can't see it! You take it, I've got you covered!"

I slowly rolled over and began a Split S with full power straight down to intercept what I thought might be a couple of MiGs headed due south. Cox, as he saw me roll over toward him, rolled into a right bank so he could visually pick me up as I crossed under. Since I had gone straight down, he didn't see me. Shark 3 called asking which way I had gone and I came right back with "Straight down. Come on down and find me!" With the G suit crushing everything toward my chest cavity, I was unable to breathe much until I leveled off

at 500ft, going like a bat out of hell.

I had found my MiG - two - nope four - whoops eight! This may be my last chance with the war winding down so as long as I'm going to do it, I may as well 'take the leader and turn the peasants loose'. With the throttle pulled back to slow my rapid overtake, I picked the leader of the first four MiGs and started to close inside of 2000 ft. Suddenly I noticed another 8 MiGs on my left. We were all at about 1000 ft. altitude looking at each other. Just then the 8 MiGs in front of me broke in all directions but down. It really hacked me. Here I had a sitting duck kill and then it was jerked right out from under me. I made MY mistake then - I threw out my speed brakes, throttled to idle, and tracked the MiG leader as I pulled the trigger. Only the ridiculous curve of my tracers, plus the gunfire rapidly slowing, clued me in as to the 'Gs' I

Maj. John Glenn - USMC, astronaut cum Senator, had three MiG kills in "MiG Mad Marine" while TDY with the 25th FIS. (NAA)

"Gopher Patrol", an F-86E-10 from the 335th FIS. 335th had more kills than any other squadron in Korea.

was pulling. I got off the trigger immediately but not before the gunsight fuse had blown!

The MiG leader reversed as I slowly began an overshoot. He and I wound up canopy to canopy, rolling around each other, each of us looking at the floor of the other's cockpit. Not daring to take my eyes off him, I suddenly saw a slight change in the MiG and with forward stick and some rudder, I slid in behind him so close I was afraid I'd hit him with my nose. He apparently had a full load of fuel as I could see it syphon slightly from the wing fuel filler caps. At point blank range, even without a sight, I would hit him each time I fired. But each time I fired, I would stall out because we were turning so tightly. Then it was a job to slowly work back through the jet wash and into position. I figure I was working from 'God awful close' to about 50 ft behind him, and at tree top level to boot!

On my 4th or 5th short burst, my aircraft was suddenly soaked with fuel as I stalled through the turn again. The next short burst caused flame to stream back around both sides and over my canopy. At this point his engine quit and I shot past him and rolled into a left turn as a MiG came in steeply from my left. When the overshoot was forced, I reversed and momentarily tried to find and use the sight. Since it was inoperable, I just held the trigger down and walked the tracers through him before he could get out of range. Rapidly looking behind, I had to take a hard left turn because I had 5 MiGs trying to cut inside me. I was fortunate enough to establish an early angle on them so they couldn't quite turn with me. By now I was being hosed heavily with cannon fire as each MiG started shooting. There were 5 of them on me and I couldn't figure out now how to turn them loose.

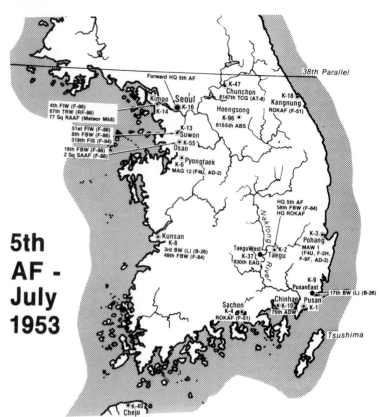

5th AF - July 1953

F-86F No.51-12941 was Col. James K. Johnson's aircraft. Col. Johnson was a double ace with 10 kills. (Brewer)

"Cochise", F-86E-1 No.50-688 from the 4th Wing, had one locomotive, 12 rail cars, 6 trucks and a MiG to its credit. (Shaw via Buchanan)

Capt. Manuel 'Pete' Fernandez leaves the runway at K-14 for a *MiG* sweep down the Yalu. 'Pete' had 14½ *MiGs* by war's end. (Miller)

Another piece of artwork applied to 4th FIW aircraft. This time having Bugs Bunny in a Sherlock Holmes hat, checking on a discharge. Note the 10 kills under the windscreen. (Garrett)

One of Fernandez's *MiGs*. (Fernandez)

Still on the deck and shooting at anything in front of me as I turned, I caused another *MiG* to splash into the ground, although I can't say whether it was a couple of hits from me or the low jet wash that did it. When the second *MiG* hit, the rest broke towards the Yalu and I fled toward K-14. Al Cox said he had seen the whole hassle from above and had been calling me through the entire fight but all I would say was "Don't bother me, I'm busy!" Al had picked up the fight visually when the *MiG* leader had burst into flame and had charged over to help. According to Al, 8 *MiGs* flew top cover while I 'entertained' the other 8. When Al showed up and the second *MiG* hit, they decided to pull out. I was ready also, not to mention the fact that I was on 'Bingo' fuel. I was credited with two *MiGs* destroyed and one damaged for the day.

Maj. Vermont Garrison
5 June 1953, F-86F No. 51-12944, 335th FIS
"Yellow Lead"

The mission for 5 June was a fighter sweep down the river. We would be Yellow Flight with myself being Yellow Lead, 1Lt. Jones in Yellow 2, Capt. Lonnie Moore in Yellow 3 and flying element lead, and 2Lt. Bill Schrimsher in Yellow 4. After takeoff and join-up, we proceeded north to the river, climbing to an altitude of 45,000 ft and checking our guns and sights as we crossed into enemy territory. We arrived on station at the mouth of the Yalu and could see the dust tracks of *MiGs* becoming airborne across the river. Yellow Flight

then crossed the river and proceeded north to Feng Cheng airfield, a known *MiG* base. We arrived over the airfield at 45,000 ft. and I observed some 30 to 40 *MiGs* taking off from the field. Too good to be true! We immediately peeled off and dove down to the attack. As we passed through 20,000 ft altitude, I observed that there were 15 or 20 *MiGs* orbiting over the field, undoubtably providing cover for those still in takeoff.

Continuing on down at a terrific closure rate, I leveled off behind two of the *MiGs* at about 500 ft. altitude and opened fire on the nearest *MiG*. Due to our speed, slightly over Mach 1, the closure rate between the *MiG* and myself was terrific. I fired a long burst hitting the *MiG* all the time and the aircraft blew up in my face. I immediately picked out a second *MiG* a little farther out and opened fire. Again, my speed let me close at a high rate. I was pouring fire into the second *MiG* all the way in. Pulling up over his right wing, I observed the *MiG* to roll over, crash and explode about 500 ft. below us. I then observed a third *MiG* turning right, just ahead and low on the tree tops. I asked Yellow 2, Lt. Jones, to take him and I would cover since I feared I was about to run out of ammo. Lt. Jones opened fire and hit the *MiG* in the aft section of his fuselage. The *MiG's* tail came off and he crashed in the hills. Capt. Moore and Lt. Schrimsher also destroyed 2 *MiGs*, one of which I saw crash and explode.

Then, the roof fell in! The *MiGs* that had been CAPing the field, that we had flown through on the way down, were now streaming down on top of us. I called "Yellow Flight, break for home!" and started talking about some cloud cover that we had seen on the way in. It was time to use any type of

Capt. Ralph Parr's last kill, and the last kill of the war, a military IL-12 transport. The Russians sued Capt. Parr in the World Court, claiming he shot down a civilian airliner. (USAF)

cover we could find to try and shake off the *MiGs*. Luckily, we had not lost much speed during the encounter and we had shaken off the *MiGs* by the time we reached the Yalu. Crossing the river, we ran straight for home - K-14. We, a flight of four, had destroyed 5 *MiGs* in less than two minutes time. I had received the only damage, some scratches and dents from pieces of the first *MiG* that had exploded in front of me.

July began with the Korean monsoon socking in both the *Sabre* and *MiG* fields until 10 July. The weather cleared enough to allow three more aces to be crowned, and another 'triple ace'. When the weather cleared on the 10th, Major John Bolt - USMC who was TDY with the 39th FIS, went north for a Yalu sweep. He was leading 'Mac' McConnell's old 'Hot Dog' Flight. When he returned, he had scored his 5th and 6th *MiG* kills to become the Navy Department's only *MiG* ace.

Major John Bolt - USMC
11 July 1953, 39th FIS, F-86F No. 51-2852, "Dog Lead"

I was assigned to the 39th FIS flying out of K-13. It was an exchange tour after flying 92 combat missions in *F9Fs* from VMF-215 at K-6. Luck was with me and I was assigned to Joe McConnell's Dog Flight, known as 'the hot dog flight'. My first eleven missions were flown on Mac's wing. But after Mac left, in May 1953, I was given command of Dog Flight.

We had been crossing the Yalu on a rather regular basis, with the greatest risk to us coming from our own brass rather than the *MiGs*. During the tailend of Mac's tour, we were getting most of our kills over and around Antung, which lies about 30 miles north of the Yalu. We used to try and provoke the *MiGs* into taking off by 'booming' the airfield or simply skimming across the field at treetop level. You were supposedly setting your watch by the clock on the Antung control tower. If you were lucky, a couple of *MiGs* would scramble and you'd get to nail them. The tower check, though was made whether any *MiGs* were taxiing or not. It was simply a way of showing the *MiG* drivers who was the boss.

On 11 July we had the afternoon mission. It was my 37th in an *F-86*. The mission was an escort of some recce planes taking pictures of Antung and the other *MiG* bases across the river. Leaving K-13, we went north, checking and clearing our guns and sights around PyongYang. As we approached the river, we really didn't know what to expect as we hadn't seen any *MiGs* in over 10 days. All of a sudden I saw them, 4 *MiGs* taking off from Antung.

"This is Dog Lead, I have bandits taking off from Antung! Dog Flight — Drop tanks!" There were four of them and two of us as my second element had to return to K-13 due to a non-transferring drop tank. Nosing down, I rolled into a Split S with the dive brakes cracked. As was my custom on entering a firing position, I test fired the guns, turned on the windshield defroster and triggered my 'G' suit.

The four *MiGs* were at about 500 feet and going full bore. Leveling off I blacked out momentarily, coming out of it about 1500 feet behind the *MiGs*. Our closure rate was so high that I was getting transonic wing roll, which made the shooting very tough indeed. Closing to 600 feet behind the second *MiG* on the left, I let go with four short bursts of fire. The *MiG* started to smoke, rolled over and crashed into the hills.

In the meantime, Dog 2, who was behind me, had taken the *MiG* leader under fire. All of a sudden this other dude, the *MiG* leader, drifted over my way. I pulled up the nose and closed to within 500 feet. I managed to get a few shots into him on the turn, and when he rolled out, I got a prolonged burst into his tailpipe. He began to burn and I was so close that I was nearly blinded by the dense smoke. I pulled out and got out of the smoke just in time. I watched as the canopy came off and the pilot ejected himself and floated to the ground. By this time, Dog 2 and I were both below 'Bingo fuel', so we turned south and headed for K-13. The whole show had taken about 5 minutes and 1200 rounds - and we got a pretty good return on the investment.

Capt. Clyde Curtin and Major Stephan Bettinger also reached the magic number of 5 to become the 38th and 39th and last aces of the Korean War. Bettinger was shot down on his 'ace' mission and his 'acedom' wasn't announced until after his release from the Red prison camp. Major James Jabara got a *MiG* on 15 July to make him the second 'triple jet ace' in history. He also was immediately grounded and sent back to the states. FEAF was taking no chances with their best.

On 22 July, Lt. Sam Young from the 51st Wing was flying a *MiG* sweep on the Yalu when four *MiGs* came across the river right below his flight. It was his first contact with the *MiGs* in 34 missions and they weren't going to get away. He shot one of the *MiGs* down for his first kill. It was the last *MiG 15* to go down in Korea during the war.

Capt. Ralph Parr would get the last kill of the war. It made him a double ace but that isn't the reason that he'll never forget that *IL-12* transport that found itself in his sights on the afternoon of 27 July.

Capt. Ralph Parr
27 July 1953, 335th FIS, F-86F No. 51-12959

Our mission for the day was an escort mission of some photo recce aircraft up near the Yalu. Hqtrs wanted some good pictures of the *MiG* fields so they could determine how many *MiGs* had been moved into North Korea. The war was

Touchdown of the last sortie by a 51st FIW *F-86* during the Korean War. Missions of the day were all *MiG* sweeps to prevent the Reds from moving *MiGs* back into North Korea. (Chapman)

Last actual mission of the war was an *RB-26* sortie from the 12th TRS, which landed at 2201 hrs, 27 July 1953. (Brewer)

Several *MiGs* have been shot down since the end of the war. Lt. Charles 'Fish' Salmon and Capt. George Williams, both of the 4th FDW, each got a *MiG* in February 1955. (USAF)

Photo taken about 5 minutes after Lt. No Kum Suk landed his NKAF *MiG 15* at K-14 in October 1953. He received a check for $100,000.00 for delivering the *MiG* into US hands. (AFM)

Table of Differences

Aircraft	Wingspan	Length	Weight	Max Speed Sea Level	Max Speed 45,000ft.	Rate of Climb	Ceiling	Range	Armament	Ammo Load
MiG 15	33.1'	36.26'	11,070lb	668mph	575mph	10,100ft/min	55,000'	675mi.	2-23mm 1-37mm	160rds 40rds
F-86E-5	37.12'	37.54'	19,346lb	679mph	582mph	7,250ft/min	48,000'	463mi.	6-.50cal	1,602rds
F-86F-30	37.12'	37.54'	17,921lb	695mph	595mph	9,300ft/min	48,000'	458mi.	6-.50cal	1,602rds

Aircraft	Rate of fire	Gunsight type	Remarks
MiG 15	650rds/min 450rds/min	Gyroscopic type	Unstable gun platform, rate of fire too slow. No radar-ranging gunsight, very fast rate of climb.
F-86E-5	1,100rds/min	Gyroscopic type	Not enough 'hitting power' in .50 calibre guns, no radar-ranging gunsight, much more armor pilot protection.
F-86F-30	1,100rds/min	Radar ranging	Big advantage in radar-ranging gunsight, '6-3' wing with fences made a very stable gun platform at high altitudes, '6-3' wing also made for more control in transonic area.

due to end at midnight and according to the negotiations, nothing was to be moved into North Korea. The military equipment that was already there, including *MiGs*, was all that was allowed to stay in North Korea.

The recce birds couldn't get any pictures because of a heavy undercast down on the river so we started back for K-14. A little south of Nami-si Dong on the Korean coast, a speck of silver caught my eye. We were flying about 30,000 feet and the bogey was way down, maybe at 10,000. I took my wingman and we went down for a look-see.

It was an *IL-12* transport, silver in color, with red stars on the fuselage and wings. I double-checked to see where in North Korea I was at the time. On this day, we definitely didn't want to be on the wrong side of the Yalu. Confirming that we were deep in North Korea, I told my wingman that I was going to take him. He was a sitting duck. I just pulled in behind him and gave him a couple of bursts. He caught fire, banked over and crashed in the hills below. That *IL-12* had probably been cutting across there for months but today he just wasn't lucky.

The war ended at midnight and I didn't think another thing about that *IL-12*. The next thing I know, I'm being called in to FEAF Hqtrs. and they're asking me about this Russian airliner that I shot down 60 miles inside Manchuria. The Reds were making a big stink about it. They did, in fact, file a lawsuit against me personally in the World Court in Holland.

The Air Force set up a full inquiry into the matter even before it was to go to World Court. I was called in, my wingman and everyone else in the flight were also called in. My gun camera film was run again and again. The questions were always the same - "Where were you? What type of aircraft was it? How was it marked? Can you prove it?" After all the evidence was in, the Air Force decided that I was in the right. The aircraft was exactly what I said, where I said, and

the kill was a legal kill. The Air Force would defend me with all this evidence when the suit came to trial in World Court.

The press had a hey-day with the investigation. The US press would say I didn't do it, the Russian press would say I did. The ending was a trifle anti-climactic. With the evidence piling up in my favor, the Russians simply dropped the suit just prior to its coming to trial. I was vindicated but it sure was one hell of a hassle for one lousy *IL-12*.

The war ended at Midnight on 27 July 1953. It had lasted a little over three years. There were still two Koreas, a North and a South. And they were still divided at roughly the 38th Parallel.

The Reds lost 954 aircraft, 827 of which were *MiG 15s*. The *Sabres* shot down 792 of that total. Air-to-air losses of US fighters included 78 *Sabres*, 14 *F-80s*, 18 *F-84s*, 10 *F-51s*, and one *F-94B*. Although there were only 17 *B-29s* lost over North Korea, there were dozens more that never flew again after making it to their home field. Even with proper escort, the *B-29s* were meat on the table for the *MiGs*. The *B-29s* themselves were too slow and the computer gunsights they were using couldn't keep up with the rapid closure rates of the *MiGs*.

The war was over but the air battles continued for many years to come. Lt. Harvey Brown, 67th FBS, tells of escorting *RB-45Cs* along the Parallel and watching the *MiGs* orbit up high. The US pilots had orders not to fire unless the *MiGs* made a firing pass on the *RB-45*. The *MiGs* did and their pass led them right through the guns of the escort flight. All four *MiGs* went down. Capt. George Williams and Lt. Charles Salmon each got a *MiG* in February 1955. Again, they were escorting an *RB-45* but this time they were off the coast of North Korea.

Korea, as much as any theater in WW2, was won by airpower. Captured Chinese documents report that it was the opinion of the Chinese General Staff that, had they gotten air superiority at any time during the war, they could have pushed the UN troops into the sea. The Fifth Air Force crews were the only obstacle that could stop it from happening. Without them, the Reds might have done it.

The *MiG 15* in full US Air Force markings at Wright-Patterson AFB for flight testing. (USAF)

MiG 15 cockpit was cramped and the gunsight was not of the radar-ranging variety. (AFM)

MiG guns were lowered from the airplane on a 'tray'. Ammo supply was not fully adequate for fighter-to-fighter combat. (USAF)

The *MiG 15* was a swept wing, high altitude bomber intercepter powered by a Soviet version of the Rolls-Royce Nene jet engine. Designed by the Mikoyan/Gurevich team, it made its first flight on 30 December 1947. Designed as a bomber intercepter, it suffered from a slow cyclic rate of fire in the air-to-air fighting in Korea. The high position of the tail made it unstable at high Mach numbers.

But the *MiG* pilot had two big advantages in Korea - a great rate of climb and the UN policy that made their bases into sanctuaries. The rate of climb for the *MiG* was 10,100ft/min, much better than the best *Sabre*, the *F-86F* at 9,300ft/min. This rate of climb, plus a service ceiling advantage of some 7,000 feet, had a great deal to do with Red air tactics.

The Reds were based at 'sanctuaries' such as Antung, Ta-ku-shan and Feng-cheng, just across the Yalu River. From these 'sanctuaries', their GCI (Ground Control Intercept) radar would scramble them to meet the *Sabres*. Climbing usually to an altitude of 50,000+ feet on the north side of the Yalu, they would then use many different attack schemes to try and gain an advantage over the *Sabres*. The "Hit and Run", "Zoom and Sun", "Staircase" and "Yo-Yo" were common and all depended upon the *MiG's* great rate of climb to keep them out of trouble.

MiG pilots came from many different countries including the Warsaw Pact, China, and of course, Russia. Sometimes they brought their own aircraft as US pilots reported seeing almost every type of Iron Curtain national insignia on the *MiGs*, including red crosses! The better Red units had, as with US units, a great deal of colorful marking. Lightning bolts, command stripes, entire tails of red, wing stripes, all were seen on the *MiGs*. One of the best units to fly in Korea was a believed-to-be Russian unit that camouflaged their aircraft in overall coppery-tan. Taking to the air in early 1953, they were much more aggressive than most Red pilots. They did shoot down some *Sabres* but were decimated and withdrawn by April 1953. The great Russian ace Kozhedub led the Red units for a year in the 1951-52 period.

Lt. Kum Suk No, who defected with his *MiG* to Kimpo in 1953, reports that Red air strength was slightly over 900 *MiGs*: 400 Russian, 400 Chinese, and two North Korean units of about 125 *MiGs*. This was faced by the American *Sabre* contingent which ran from 7 aircraft in December 1950, to six squadrons in 1952, to twelve squadrons, about 300 *F-86s*, at war's end. Lt. No further reports that the Reds lost over 800 planes and pilots by war's end. His division of 70 *MiGs* lost 30.

Lt. No makes the flat statement that, "But for the sheer superiority of the American *Sabre*, I'm sure the Korean War would still be going on today." This author wishes to add that all airplanes, no matter how good, still need a pilot and the American pilot is 'Second To None'.

Capt. Richard Creighton landing at K-14 in his *F-86A-5*. He shot down 5 *MiGs*. (USAF)

Major James Jabara relaxes in the cockpit after landing following his last kill of the war - 15 July 1953. 'Jabby' used many different aircraft during his two tours in Korea. (Hendle)

NAME	RANK	KILLS	DATE		TYPE
James Jabara	Capt.	1.0	4	03 51	MIG15
334 SQ		1.0	4	10 51	MIG15
		1.0	4	12 51	MIG15
		1.0	4	22 51	MIG15
		2.0	5	20 51	MIG15
	Maj.	1.0	5	16 53	MIG15
		2.0	5	26 53	MIG15
		2.0	6	10 53	MIG15
		1.0	6	18 53	MIG15
		2.0	6	30 53	MIG15
		1.0	7	15 53	MIG15

The nose of Maj. James Jabara's last aircraft showing his full score. (Hendle)

Col. Royal Baker's "Angel Face and The Babes". Col. Baker was CO of the 4th Wing when he shot down 13 *MiGs*. (Shaw via Buchanan)

NAME		RANK	KILLS	DATE			TYPE
Royal N. Baker	336 SQ	Col.	1.0	6	20	52	LA9
			1.0	7	04	52	MIG15
	335 SQ		1.0	11	01	52	MIG15
			1.0	11	17	52	MIG15
	336 SQ		1.0	10	25	52	MIG15
	335 SQ		1.0	12	07	52	MIG15
			0.5	12	07	52	MIG15
			0.5	12	16	52	MIG15
	336 SQ		1.0	1	13	53	MIG15
	335 SQ		1.0	1	21	53	MIG15
			1.0	2	14	53	MIG15
			1.0	2	19	53	MIG15
			1.0	3	08	53	MIG15
			1.0	3	13	53	MIG15

Capt. Lonnie Moore carried the name of his wife "Margie" on the right side of his aircraft, and his son's name, "Billie", on the left. He ended the war with 10 *MiGs*. (NAA)

Capt. Bob Love's "Bernie's Bo" in which he got 6 *MiGs*. (USAF)

Capt. Manuel 'Pete' Fernandez inflight over Korea. Note the 8 kills on the starboard nose belonging to the aircraft. (USAF)

NAME	RANK	KILLS	DATE			TYPE
Manuel J. Fernandez, Jr.	Capt.	1.0	10	04	52	MIG15
		1.0	11	20	52	MIG15
334 SQ		1.0	12	16	52	MIG15
		1.0	1	14	53	MIG15
		1.0	2	18	53	MIG15
		1.0	2	18	53	MIG15
		1.0	3	09	53	MIG15
		1.0	3	14	53	MIG15
		2.0	3	21	53	MIG15
		1.0	4	17	53	MIG15
		1.0	5	08	53	MIG15
		1.0	5	16	53	MIG15
		1.0	5	10	53	MIG15
		0.5	5	10	53	MIG15

'Pete' Fernandez by his second aircraft, showing his full score. (Miller)

FU-830 was Capt. Fernandez's first aircraft, which was wrecked while he was on R&R in Japan. (USAF)

'The Gang' representing 54 *MiGs* - (from left) Lonnie Moore - 10 *MiGs*, Vermont Garrison - 10 *MiGs*, James K. Johnson - 10 *MiGs*, Ralph Parr - 9 *MiGs* and James Jabara - 15 *MiGs*. (USAF)

4th FIW team at the 1953 FEAF Gunnery Meet. The first aircraft belonged to Vermont Garrison, an *F-86F*. The second aircraft was piloted by Ralph Parr but it was not his combat aircraft, even though it carried his full score. (USAF)

Maj. Frederick Blesse got 10 *MiGs* in *F-86E-10* No.51-2821.(Miller)

'306 *MiGs* Down' sign held by various pilots in the 4th FIW - December 1951. The aircraft "Mary & The Js" is Col. Harrison Thyng's *F-86E* No. 50-623. (USAF)

Maj. Donald Adams, 13th Ace in Korea, congratulates Capt. Robert Latshaw, the 14th Ace. They stand by Capt. Latshaw's aircraft, *F-86E* No. 50-632. (USAF)

'Mac' walks away from the second "Beautious Butch" after getting No. 16. Note the kill marks are *MiG* symbols - 18 May 1953. (Chapman)

'Mac' in the cockpit of "Beauteous Butch II" on 19 May 1953. Aircraft was repainted overnight for press pictures, now having 'star kills' and the name mis-spelled "Beauteous". (USAF)

Capt. Joseph McConnell by his first "Beautious Butch", an *F-86E* No. 51-2753 that was shot from under him on 12 May 1953. (USAF)

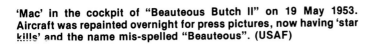

NAME	RANK	KILLS	DATE		TYPE
Joseph M. McConnell Jr.,	1st Lt.	1.0	1	14 53	MIG15
		1.0	1	21 53	MIG15
39 SQ		1.0	1	30 53	MIG15
		1.0	1	31 53	MIG15
		1.0	2	16 53	MIG15
		1.0	3	08 53	MIG15
		1.0	3	14 53	MIG15
		1.0	4	12 53	MIG15
	Capt.	1.0	4	16 53	MIG15
		1.0	4	24 53	MIG15
		1.0	5	13 53	MIG15
		1.0	5	15 53	MIG15
		1.0	5	16 53	MIG15
		2.0	5	18 53	MIG15
		1.0	5	18 53	MIG15

"Beauteous Butch II" in a revetment at K-13, 19 May 1953. Note blue nose flash, also carried on drop tank noses. (Menard)

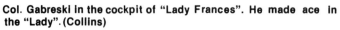

Col. Gabreski in the cockpit of "Lady Frances". He made ace in the "Lady". (Collins)

"Darling Dottie" is Maj. John Bolt's aircraft. A Marine pilot TDY with the 39th FIS, Maj. Bolt got 6 *MiGs* and was the only non-Air Force *MiG* ace. (Bolt)

"Glory-Us", the *F-86E* of Lt Peter Frederick of the 336th FIS. Lt. Frederick shot down 3 *MiGs.* (Baker)

"MiG Mad Mavis", the personal mount of LtCol. George Ruddell, CO of the 39th FIS. Col. Ruddell shot down 8 *MiGs*. (NAA)

Capt. Harold Fischer's "Paper Tiger" in which he shot down 10 *MiGs*. Capt. Fischer spent over 2 years in a Chinese prison camp when he was shot down and ended up on the wrong side of the Yalu. (USAF)

Lt. Henry Buttlemann, at 24 the youngest ace in Korea. He shot down 6 *MiGs* in *F-86F* No.51-2890. Note the new "U.S. Air Force" logo on the fuselage side, introduced in June 1953. (Chapman)

Mig Maulers

KOREAN WAR
1950-1953

CAPT. J.D.McCONNELL, JR.
27 TH JET ACE
16 MIGS

MAJ. J.JABARA
1ST JET ACE
15 MIGS

CAPT. M.J.FERNANDEZ
26 TH JET ACE
14 MIGS

CAPT. R.N.BAKER
21ST JET ACE
12 MIGS, I LA-9

MAJ. G.A.DAVIS
5TH JET ACE
11 MIGS

LT. H.E.FISCHER
25TH JET ACE
10 MIGS

COL. J.K.JOHNSON
29TH JET ACE
10 MIGS

CAPT. R.S.PARR
33RD JET ACE
10 MIGS

LT. JAMES F.LOW
17TH JET ACE
9 MIGS

MAJ. F.C.BLESSE
19TH JET ACE
9 MIGS, I LA-9

CAPT. L.R.MOORE
34TH JET ACE
9 MIGS, I LA-9

CAPT. R.RISNER
20TH JET ACE
8 MIGS

MAJ. V.GARRISON
32ND JET ACE
8 MIGS

CAPT. C.D.JOLLEY
18TH JET ACE
7 MIGS

CAPT. L.W.LILLEY
22ND JET ACE
7 MIGS

LT. H.BUTTLEMAN
36TH JET ACE
7 MIGS

COL. F.S.GABRESKI
8TH JET ACE
6 1/2 MIGS

CAPT. D.E.ADAMS
14 TH JET ACE
6 1/2 MIGS

MAJ. J.P.HAGERSTROM
28TH JET ACE
6 1/2 MIGS

COL. G.L.JONES
30TH JET ACE
6 1/2 MIGS

CAPT. I.C.KINCHELOE
10TH JET ACE
5 MIGS - 4 YAK-9

CAPT. R.J.LOVE
11TH JET ACE
6 MIGS

MAJ. J.F.BOLT
37TH JET ACE
6 MIGS

LT. J.H.KASLER
15TH JET ACE
6 MIGS

MAJ. W.T.WHISNER
7TH JET ACE
5 1/2 MIGS

CAPT. R.S.BECKER
2ND JET ACE
5 MIGS

CAPT. R.GIBSON
3 RD JET ACE
5 MIGS

LT COL. R.D.CREIGHTON
4 TH JET ACE
5 MIGS

CAPT. R.H.MOORE
9TH JET ACE
5 MIGS

MAJ. W.H.WESCOTT
12 TH JET ACE
5 MIGS

CAPT. R.T.LATSHAW
13 TH JET ACE
5 MIGS

COL. H.R.THYNG
16 TH JET ACE
5 MIGS

LT. C.G.FOSTER
23RD JET ACE
5 MIGS

CAPT. D.W.OVERTON III
24 TH JET ACE
5 MIGS

LT. COL. G.L.RUDDELL
31ST JET ACE
5 MIGS

COL. R.P.BALDWIN
35 TH JET ACE
5 MIGS

CAPT. C.A.CURTIN
38 TH JET ACE
5 MIGS

MAJ. S.L.BETTINGER
39 TH JET
5 MIGS

MAJ. W.W.MARSHALL
4 1/2 MIGS - 1 TU-2 Ia